D1825743

Beyond Buildings

Beyond Buildings:
Designed Spaces as Visual Persuasion

By

J. Donald Ragsdale

Beyond Buildings: Designed Spaces as Visual Persuasion,
by J. Donald Ragsdale

This book first published 2014

Cambridge Scholars Publishing

12 Back Chapman Street, Newcastle upon Tyne, NE6 2XX, UK

British Library Cataloguing in Publication Data
A catalogue record for this book is available from the British Library

ISBN (10): 1-4438-5634-7, ISBN (13): 978-1-4438-5634-8

TABLE OF CONTENTS

LIST OF FIGURES

Some figures were obtained from commons.wikimedia.org and were contributed to this public domain depository by the following:

2-1 Boboli Gardens, ingorrr, no date.
2-2 Villa d'Este, mmxbass, 4/8/2005.
2-3 Villa Lante, Roberto Ferrari, 4/25/2007.
2-4 Vaux le Vicomte, Jebulon, 9/5/2010.
2-5 Versailles, Michael Plasmeier, 7/4/2006.
2-6 Castle Howard, Gordon Hatton, 5/18/2009.
2-7 Stowe, Philip Halling, 6/7/2008.
2-8 Stourhead, Delta 51, 7/27/2011.

Figure 3-16, Bellingrath Gardens, is by Frances Brandau-Brown. Figures 4-7, Bryce Canyon Hoodoos, and 9-12, Hall of Mirrors, are by Sandy Irwin Ragsdale. All other images are by the author.

ACKNOWLEDGEMENTS

As in my previous four volumes on visual persuasion published by Cambridge Scholars Publishing, I wish to acknowledge my debt to a number of people. There are the historical influences: my college and graduate school professors, my chairs and deans in various places of employment, and my professional colleagues. Then there is the vital travel support afforded me by Sam Houston State University. Andy Nercessian and Amanda Millar at Cambridge Scholars Publishing have respectively endorsed my ideas and edited my manuscripts. Last, there is my family—Sandy, Paul, Alan, Katie, Mike, Amy, Sydney, and Tristen. Thank you one and all.

Abbreviated versions of Chapters Two and Seven of this book have appeared previously: Ragsdale, J. D., and F. E. Brandau-Brown. 2013. Space exploration: Assessing designed spaces as visual persuasion. *The International Journal of Arts Theory and History, 7,* 29-39, and Ragsdale, J. D., and F. E. Brandau-Brown. 2013. Designing urban spaces for visual impact: Ancient Athens and Rome. *The International Journal of Civic, Political, and Community Studies, 10,* 51-58, both published by Common Ground Publishing. Chapters Five and Seven, as noted in the book itself, were co-authored with my colleague Frances E. Brandau-Brown.

PREFACE

This book is a natural extension of previous ones which I have written or edited on the subject of visual persuasion. Those books addressed the visual impact of structures. Two, for example, focused on art museums and demonstrated how a museum's collection and its arrangement of the collection were deliberate means of visual influence. Additionally, those books examined the museums' architecture as a separate type of visual persuasion. The most recent book assessed architecture in general, considering a wide range of buildings and structures such as skyscrapers, palaces, places of residence, government buildings, universities, and, again, museums.

Assessing architecture necessitated a consideration of design elements that were not part of the structure itself. An important element of architecture, for example, is a building site. It is as important to note the placement of a structure such as the Louvre as it is to consider its architectural style. The location of the Louvre at one end of the grand axis known as the Champs Élysées, as well as the museum's centrality in the city of Paris, are both elements which contribute powerfully to the visual power of the building. The grounds of such palaces as Versailles and Schönbrunn equally illustrate the visual power of site.

This book focuses specifically on the designed spaces which are a part of buildings as well as spaces, such as parks and gardens, which have been created as means of visual influence in and of themselves. It seeks first to find those visual images, elements, and communication principles which would be appropriate in answering the questions of how designed spaces influence viewers and to what degree. Secondly, it considers a variety of such spaces, such as parks, gardens, national parks, zoological gardens, battlefields, and even cities. Finally, the book examines a sample of especially notable interior spaces as examples of visual persuasion.

In the four previous books, I focused on those places I had actually visited, studied at first hand, and photographed, believing that there is no satisfactory substitute for the writer's actual presence. In this book, however, it was not possible to visit every place. Time and limited funds precluded that, especially with respect to US national parks and American battlefield memorials, cemeteries, and monuments outside the US. However, each such place assessed within was studied carefully through photographs and videos readily available online.

Also like my previous books on visual persuasion, this is a scholarly work, which concerns itself principally with theory and its application in the assessment of specific items. However like the previous books, this one should also be of value to the casual reader and especially the traveler as a point of reference to enhance visits to one or more of the designed spaces examined within.

CHAPTER ONE

THREE APPROACHES TO STUDYING SPACE AS VISUAL PERSUASION

"Space is an exceedingly common commodity: It fills the universe and surrounds us throughout our lives. It can appear so thin and extended that the sense of dimension is numbed or so richly infused with a three-dimensional presence that it endows everything within its fold with special meaning. Intensely three-dimensional space has the remarkable capacity to enhance our lives. It imparts our surroundings with a pleasing sense of comfort and security that is as important to the enjoyment of life as sunlight and a place to rest. It is a basic component of good urban design" (Hedman & Jaszewski 1984, 53). An examination of designed spaces is the central concern of this book, which assessment has the purpose of determining how such spaces impact the viewer visually. The power of space to affect viewers noted by Hedman and Jaszewski is akin to that of buildings and other structures and falls into the general concept of visual persuasion. This book is a natural and direct extension of previous studies of structures in general (Ragsdale 2007), American art museums (Ragsdale 2009a), Western European art museums (Ragsdale 2009b), and architecture as a whole (Ragsdale 2011) as visual persuasion. For that reason, it is appropriate to begin here with a brief account of how scholars with diverse backgrounds have approached the evaluation of visual persuasion. There are generally three such approaches: the visual rhetoric approach, the semiotic, and, for want of a better term, the elemental.

The study of persuasion has been the purview of scholars, especially those in communication studies, since Classical times and perhaps earlier. It has been overwhelmingly a study of verbal behavior under the rubric of rhetoric. Rhetoric has usually been associated with speakers, and at its heart has been about finding, as Aristotle put it, "the available means of persuasion" (1954, 24). Persuasion, in turn, referred primarily to changing someone's way of thinking or behaving or both.

Examples abound. A common one would be found in those speeches, advertisements, and tracts which seek to convince smokers that smoking may lead to lung cancer or emphysema and to get them to quit. The process by which persuasion takes place is one which at its heart is quite simple: someone offers an assertion, which is to say makes a claim. Then this person provides some form of warrant or proof for that assertion or claim. The proof may be a fact, an example, testimony, and the like. Usually, there are several warrants provided.

Of course, the actual process of persuasion is not so simple. Sometimes, an appeal to an emotion such as patriotism substitutes for the logical warrants mentioned above, and sometimes assertions or claims may be made without providing any proof but which are effective because of the credibility ascribed to the source by the audience. There is also an awareness by students of persuasion that efforts to persuade depend almost entirely on how that audience's prior attitudes, values, and beliefs interact with the claims and warrants, a recognition that one cannot be persuaded unless one wants to be.

Especially helpful in understanding certain forms of visual persuasion is an awareness of what might be called incidental or unintentional persuasion. An example might be a single fact encountered by an auditor in a news report or overheard among friends. Let's say it is a statement that a principal cause of gum disease is the failure to use dental floss twice a day. That fact alone may be sufficient for the auditor to begin systematic flossing. It is not necessary that there be a full-blown persuasive speech or an ad campaign for persuasion to take place. In visual persuasion, a viewer may encounter an image completely separate from any kind of specific effort to have influence. Architecture is a good visual analogy of incidental persuasion. Subsequently, the issue of just what kind of response it is that one has to a standalone visual image will be explored, but clearly the response is not merely passivity. Previously, the response has been called compelling (Ragsdale 2011).

Although strongly committed to the position that rhetoric is at heart a verbal discipline, there have recently been those in the field who have embraced the notion that visual phenomena are also persuasive. Studies of visual persuasion by these scholars are called visual rhetoric. Although often referred to as rhetorical theory, the rhetorical approach is not theoretical in any scientific sense. To the layman, it might be described as the application of some philosophical perspective to the explanation of rhetorical phenomena. Aristotle (1954), for example, identified what he observed to be the essential components of oral persuasion, identifying such things as logic, emotion, and source credibility to mention the most fundamental ones.

Through the centuries, scholars not only have adapted Aristotle's views to the teaching of public speaking but have also used his categories as an analytical tool for assessing speeches. In the 20th century, Kenneth Burke (1955) observed that seeking to ingratiate oneself with an audience was an essential ingredient of persuasion and that assessing rhetorical events required proper consideration of all of the elements of the events. Of course, scholars have engaged in an extensive set of Burkean analyses of speeches and speakers. Almost anyone who has written philosophically about communication may be used to provide some kind of insight into rhetorical events, and thus one regularly encounters assessments based on the texts of such recent writers as Jürgen Habermas, Jacques Lacan, Michel Foucault, Jacques Derrida, and Chaïm Perelman to name only a few.

The observation that the rhetorical approach is not theoretical in a scientific sense is not meant to be disparaging. Rather it is intended to explain the wide diversity which characterizes visual rhetorical studies as well as traditional verbal ones. Visual rhetoric, however, is not only characterized by varied approaches but is also diverse in the targets it examines. A recent volume of essays, *Defining Visual Rhetorics* (Hill and Helmers 2004, 21), acknowledges quite a variety: "political conventions, editorial pages, movie theatres, art museums, suburban food stores, government documents, as well as the Victorian drawing room and, as in Goggin's examination of needlepoint, orphanage schools in the 19th century."

While there is no typical approach, studies by Edwards (2004) and Tange (2004) give some insight into the point of view of visual rhetoricians. Edwards was interested in how "images disseminated in connection with newsworthy events become attached to the event in the form of cultural remembering. . . . some images are routinely re-presented long past the time when they are actually 'happening,' creating through visual equivalence a new experience that calls forth the reminder of the depicted event" (179). Edwards's prime example of this phenomenon is the photograph of John F. Kennedy, Jr., age 3, saluting the coffin of his slain father as it passed on its way to Arlington National Cemetery. She provides evidence of the enduring power of this image through newspaper editorial cartoons which appeared many years later at the death of JFK, Jr. She concludes that "the frequent invoking of the 'salute' photograph as well as other historical images of Kennedy and his family members served to justify coverage [of the death] by positioning the plane crash as part of a larger narrative that involved a nation, as well as a family" (193).

Tange (2004) was interested in how the concept of home among the middle classes in Victorian England "was defined in large part through the imaginative value of domesticity, [where] the physical images presented by actual homes were complemented with print images in texts that participated in creating domestic ideology" (277). To illustrate her premise, Tange provides paintings of domestic scenes, floor plans of

Victorian homes showing the residents' "places," illustrations of work tables and chairs, sketches of drawing rooms, and drawings of table settings and menus. With the proliferation of these print images, Tange points out that "readers could consume as many works as it took for domestic ideals to become second nature, so that eventually the well-read, middle-class consumer . . . might 'naturally' be able to display a properly domesticated identity" (296).

Recently, in addition to the Hill and Helmers (2004) collection of essays, other works with a visual rhetoric approach have appeared, which illustrate how the approach is developing and how interest in visual rhetoric is growing. One of these is a reader with a collection of 20 recently published essays (Olson, Finnegan, and Hope 2008). The essays "investigate a variety of visual forms—photography, editorial cartoons, public monuments, tattoos, mural art, television news and advertising, stamps, prints. They describe images doing the work of social control and of social protest or political change" (Benson 2008, 416). The editors reveal that they had in mind a textbook for a college-level course in visual rhetoric. The essays are very much in keeping with the pattern established in the Hill and Helmers collection.

Another book represents a bit of a departure from these two collections by focusing on displays, including iconic photographs, national park landscapes, Budapest's Stalin Monument, public demonstrations, and tattoos. In fact, however, the use of the term "display" is only for the purpose of emphasizing the choice rhetors make when deciding what to reveal visually and what not to. In practice, the displays under consideration are the same or quite similar to the images in the two earlier collections, and "the rhetorical study of displays proceeds from the central idea that whatever they make manifest or appear is the culmination of selective processes that constrain the range of possible meanings available to those who encounter them" (Prelli 2006, 2).

A third book is entitled *Shaping Information: The Rhetoric of Visual Conventions* (Kostelnick and Hassett 2003), but it is quite different from the previous ones mentioned here in the visual images with which it is concerned. This book is more narrowly focused on the nature of visual language itself rather than rhetoric and in particular on the charts, graphs, icons, and the like which are used as the conventions of textual illustrations. This book is a descriptive one which traces the historical development of visual images used as illustrations. Since it does not seek to provide a rhetorical perspective to the use of visual images, it is an interesting but tangential contribution to the visual rhetoric approach.

Studies of visual rhetoric provide many meaningful insights into the phenomena they examine and help in understanding the purposeful use of visual images and its likely effects. Typically, however, visual rhetoric does not delve into the semiotics of images nor the elements on which the images are based. Again, this observation is not meant to disparage studies in visual rhetoric so much as it is to distinguish them from two other approaches to the study of visual persuasion: the semiotic and the elemental. Both of these approaches are rather more interested in visual images *qua* visual images. They seek to dissect images themselves to see how they function as available means of persuasion. The second or semiotic approach focuses holistically on visual signs, while the third concerns itself with the basic elements of visual imagery—dots, lines, geometric figures, and the like—and their organization into communication strategies.

The semiotic approach to visual persuasion was developed by Paul Messaris (1997) and was primarily targeted at the wide use of visual means to influence consumers in advertising. In an effort to explain the role of visual images in influencing consumers, Messaris took a semiotic approach, specifically an adaptation of the sign system of Charles S. Peirce (Buchler 1955). Pierce's system included a wide range of signs, some of which were visual in nature. From these, Messaris selected two for a typology of visual persuasion. They were icons and indexes. Icons are *representational,* in that they look like that for which they stand. Icons are abundant in the portal sculptures of Gothic cathedrals as well as the paintings hanging in the world's art museums. Indexes are *documentary.* They are direct evidence of a thing, such as unaltered photographs and artifacts like a cannon acting as a battlefield memorial. Messaris recognized also that how a sign is interpreted often depends upon its juxtaposition to other signs. The theory of *montage* in film is an example of this juxtapositional effect. Messaris termed this phenomenon syntactic indeterminacy, and it has been used to explain such persuasive effects as those of the great dinosaur skeleton in the rotunda of The British Museum of Natural History (Ragsdale 2007) and the location in the Louvre of *Nike of Samothrace* at the head of a grand staircase (Ragsdale 2009b).

How do icons have a persuasive effect? How do they influence consumers to purchase an advertised product, or to switch from one brand to another, or to maintain their brand loyalty? Messaris (1997) begins his answer to these questions by pointing out that advertisements are unwanted forms of communication, i.e., they are not sought out by ordinary persons. For this reason, then, the first function of an icon is to get attention, and Messaris devotes considerable space to providing examples of attention-getting images. These examples include images that distort physical reality, such as an image of a woman's face with her mouth erased. The second function is to arouse an emotional response to the advertisement's product, such as the use of high or low camera angles to suggest inferiority or superiority. The desired result is influence on the viewer's attitudes and beliefs.

Indexes are also icons, but they have the added power of appearing to be real or to be representing reality faithfully. As such, indexes have the additional ability to prove something. As an example, Messaris (1997) mentions an ad for a laundry detergent. The ad shows two stained cloths immersed in solutions of different brands of detergent, with the one dipped in the product being advertised coming out cleaner than the other one. Indexes, then, offer proof analogous to the facts, statistics, and testimony of verbal persuasion, although to be sure viewers in general have come to be suspicious of staged, manipulated, or altered images especially as the awareness of the power of digital imaging has increased.

Icons and indexes are visual signs. Syntactic indeterminacy, by contrast, has to do with the arrangement or juxtaposition of signs. Syntactic indeterminacy highlights the fact that, unlike the words in a sentence, a pairing or sequence of images is missing any information to determine what the relationship is between the images. Viewers, then, are left to form an association between them based on their juxtaposition. In the famous shower sequence in Alfred Hitchcock's film *Psycho,* the viewer sees an attacker wielding a large knife followed by a woman in the shower raising her arms to repel the attack leading finally to blood in the water circling the drain. The blade never actually touches the woman's skin, but the juxtaposition of the images and the rapid cutting of the montage sequence convince the viewer otherwise.

In advertising, some claims would be impossible to make verbally, because they are false. They can, however, be suggested by the association of one image with another. An obvious example is the use of a bodybuilder demonstrating an exercise machine. It cannot be claimed that the machine was the cause of the bodybuilder's physique, since diet plays a large role in the outcome of exercise. The association between the two, though, is compelling for the uncritical viewer. When the British Museum of Natural History, as mentioned earlier, displays a huge dinosaur skeleton in its entrance rotunda, a claim is being made about the importance of the theory of evolution and without saying a word.

In both the rhetorical and the semiotic approaches, the explanation of visual persuasion is straightforward. A claim is made and an image is used as its support or warrant, such that visual and verbal persuasion differ only in their form. If the image is compelling, just as one could say a statistic is compelling, then the claim may be convincing or motivating. Of course, many variables determine the effectiveness of a persuasive appeal, but insofar as this example is confined to just one variable then it can reasonably be thought of as accurate. In some notable and widespread cases, however, visual persuasion is not comparable to the claim and warrant model mentioned above, and in these cases the rhetorical and semiotic approaches are inadequate. In these cases, and buildings are good examples of them, there is no claim unless it is an implicit one, nor is there a warrant unless the elements of visual design are warrants. In any case, it would only be artificial to try to impose the claim and warrant model on something like a building, when a much more useful approach would be to develop an approach directly suited to the image or images.

In three previous books, Ragsdale (2007, 2009a, 2009b) adapted Messaris's (1997) analysis of icons, indexes, and syntactic indeterminacy to the assessment of museums as visual persuasion. Ragsdale first used icons and indexes as the basis of a typology of museums, with art museums generally identified as iconic and museums of natural science identified as indexical. Then, the assessment of individual museums was made by evaluating the significance of the museum's collection—its icons, its indexes, or both—the significance of the works' display or "hanging"—syntactic indeterminacy—and the power of the museum's architecture. This assessment called for an expansion of Messaris's images beyond icons, indexes, and syntactic indeterminacy and for a new, elemental approach to evaluating the architecture as visual persuasion based on the elements and communication strategies of visual literacy. Subsequently, this approach was used to assess architecture in general, including palaces, residences, skyscrapers, cathedrals, universities, and the like (Ragsdale 2011).

It is this latter methodology that forms the third or elemental approach to the study of visual persuasion. Before focusing on the nature of the elemental approach, however, it will be helpful to examine the ways in which Ragsdale expanded Messaris's (1997) system. As mentioned, it was necessary to expand Messaris's system to account for structures in general and museums and their contents (Ragsdale 2007). The basic system did not, for example, afford a way to assess the difference between *discursive* and *nondiscursive* visual signs. Discursive signs have a clear parallel in language, as in the case of the "sermons in stone" of the portal iconography at Notre-Dame de Paris. However, the light-gathering structure of a cathedral, probably intended to represent the nature of God himself or of Heaven, seemed not to have any parallel in language. The term nondiscursive was used to describe such visual elements. Color is a nondiscursive sign. Space is similarly a nondiscursive sign. The ruins at Oradour-sur-Glane near Limoges in France and the tranquility of a Shinto shrine must be considered within their encompassing contexts. It was also necessary to resort to the distinction between central and peripheral pathways for information processing made in the Elaboration Likelihood Model of Petty and Cacioppo (1986). Central processing involves deliberative thought about the content of a message, while peripheral processing is more impressionistic. This distinction was especially useful in describing the differences between discursive and nondiscursive visual signs. Discursive ones would seem to necessitate central processing, while nondiscursive ones are likely to be processed peripherally.

It was also necessary to add to icons and indexes another pair of visual signs to account for the varieties of art found in museums (Ragsdale 2009a). There are inadequacies in the icon/index categorization raised by the existence in the vast majority of art objects of symbolism. A recognition of such a symbolic image is to be found in C. S. Peirce's theory of verbal signs. For Peirce, a symbol was a conventionalized representation of its object. The best example is a word, such as "man." By contrast, a stick figure drawing of a man is an icon, and a photograph of a man is an index. What, then, is a visual symbol in Peircean terms? While it might be more difficult in visual communication to find instances than in verbal communication, where symbols abound, there are conventionalized visual symbols to be found in every culture (Ragsdale 2007). Trees of life, owls, crucifixes, angels, and the like all have implications beyond mere representation. Accepting that visual signs may be symbolic provides a means for interpreting the many instances of traditional art, which are merely puzzling when contemplated as icons. So symbols not only get attention and evoke conventional emotional associations as icons do, they also carry with them specific meanings.

Peirce did not anticipate the rise of modern art and its practical rejection of representation. The works of such painters as Jackson Pollock, Wassily Kandinsky, and Piet Mondrian cannot be classified as either icons or indexes. Neither can they be called symbols. For this reason, a fourth sign is required, which has been called a *presentation*. A presentation is a visual composition of dots, lines, tones, colors, and the like presented through visual communicative strategies such as balance, symmetry, sharpness, randomness, and the like, but which does not "represent" anything. The interpretation of a presentation will always be subject to more variation than that of a symbol, an icon, or an index, since presentations do not have clearly differentiated objects. Objects of presentations are ordinarily unknowable, ineffable, or indecipherable, and their persuasive impact is likely to be a function of subjective interpretation.

Consideration of the presentation is, in fact, the point where the need for a third approach to visual persuasion became evident. Not only are works of modern art presentations, so are buildings. How does one account for the power of architecture to compel a persuasive reaction? Since buildings are not symbols, or icons, or indexes, one is forced to examine the most basic elements of architectural design themselves. This elemental approach is presented in detail in *Compelling Form* (Ragsdale 2011), therefore it will be presented here in a more summary form.

Those who are familiar with the field of linguistics are aware that language is formed by a set of fundamental building blocks called phones or sounds. Sounds are roughly indicated by an alphabet, although conventional alphabets are not good indicators of pronunciation. For that information, linguists rely on the International Phonetic Alphabet, where each symbol always and faithfully represents one and the same sound regardless of language. From these fundamental building blocks, words are built, and words are arranged into phrases and sentences. While linguists usually stop their analysis at this point, others interested in language, such as writers and literary theorists, continue to consider combinations of sentences into paragraphs, paragraphs into chapters, and so on. Semioticians, of course, focus on the denotations and connotations of words.

Like linguists, architects design buildings using fundamental building blocks. These include scale, line, rhythm, light, texture, color, ornament, acoustics, space, mass, and the like, which are combined into geometric shapes, arches, columns, domes, walls, windows, and so on (Ching 1979; Ragsdale 2011; Roth 1993; Strickland 2001). Before proceeding, one more example from the field of linguistics will be useful. From acoustic phonetics, we know that phones or sounds are actually not the fundamental units of language, although to be sure they are the fundamental perceptual units. In fact, phones are composed of basic aspects of sound which are the consequences of the production of sounds themselves. These basic aspects are called distinctive features. A simple example of a distinctive feature is voicing, which makes it possible to distinguish between such English language sounds as "p" and "b," "t" and "d," and "k" and "g." In each of these three pairs, the second sound is distinguishable from the first significantly because it is articulated with the vocal folds vibrating.

Of course, phoneticians and speech pathologists have long analyzed sounds at this more basic level. Even before the findings in acoustic phonetics using the sound spectrograph made them precise and discrete, issues of voicing, resonance, and articulatory position have been vital to an understanding of articulation and of a variety of communication disorders. To return to the elements of architecture, further probing shows that elements such as rhythm and mass resolve into yet more basic units, like dots, lines, and shapes. Often referred to as the elements of visual literacy (Dondis 1973), it is these elements that ultimately explain the visual images we see and which either do or do not have a persuasive effect on us. As sounds or phones underlie spoken language, so "the dot, line, shape, direction, tone, color, texture, dimension, scale, movement" underlie visual communication (Dondis 1973, 39).

"The dot is the simplest, irreducibly minimum unit of visual communication. . . . dots connect and therefore capable of leading the eye" (Dondis 1973, 40-41). A chain of dots is a line, which "because of its nature, has enormous energy. It is never static; it is the restless, probing, visual element of the sketch" (43). Dondis's claims seem almost fanciful and open to dispute until one finds that her observations rest on findings in the psychology of perception, especially that of Gestalt psychology.

Gestalt psychology has contributed a substantial amount to our understanding of how human perception of visual elements and communication strategies works. It suggests that there are universal human perceptual responses, such that an analysis of visual design should suggest why some images are compelling and some not. "One factor alone is common currency between artist and audience, in fact, among all people—the physical system of their visual perceptions, the psychophysiological components of the nervous system, the mechanical workings, the sensory apparatus through which they see" (Dondis 1973, 21).

With Gestalt psychology in mind, then, it is easier to accept such claims as "the square has associated with it dullness, honesty, straightness, and workmanlike meaning; the triangle, action, conflict, tension; the circle endlessness, warmth, protection" (Dondis 1973, 44). This is not the place for a primer on visual literacy, rather the purpose here is to establish the notions that basic visual elements are perceived similarly by all human beings and that they have both emotional and intellectual consequences. This said, it is reasonable to expect that an assessment of designs using these elements as units of analysis would be fruitful in discovering the reasons for their effectiveness or lack thereof as means of visual persuasion.

Basic elements are not used in isolation but rather in combinations to formulate visual messages. This happens through the application of "visual techniques" or "communication strategies." Dondis (1973, 16) discusses a number of the most common of these communication strategies but points out that there are undoubtedly many more. Some of the most common are as follows:

- Balance—Instability
- Symmetry—Asymmetry
- Regularity—Irregularity
- Simplicity—Complexity
- Unity—Fragmentation
- Economy—Intricacy
- Understatement—Exaggeration
- Predictability—Spontaneity
- Boldness—Subtlety
- Simplicity—Complexity
- Depth—Flatness
- Sharpness—Diffusion
- Sequentiality—Randomness
- Repetition—Episodicity

It might be tempting to treat these bipolar opposites as continua representing "good" versus "bad" visual messages. For example, terms like symmetry, simplicity, and sharpness seem superficially to be goals of effective design. However, there are messages that may call for something between the two poles or even full-blown asymmetry, complexity, and diffusion. The communication strategies are therefore descriptive rather than prescriptive, and each visual design, when assessed, must be evaluated in its own terms. Although it is not the focus of this book, abstract art is an especially good example of this caveat.

Dondis (1973) uses the strategies to characterize architectural styles and in doing so demonstrates how they might be used to assess other types of visual designs. Two examples should demonstrate sufficiently her approach. Classicism is a very familiar architectural style, and Dondis (140) describes it with these visual communication strategies: harmony, simplicity, accuracy, symmetry, sharpness, monochromaticity, depth, consistency, stasis, and unity. Notice that some of the terms used to describe Classicism do not appear in Dondis's list above of the most common ones, illustrating the flexibility of the use of strategies as a descriptive tool.

Expressionism is less familiar. It sought to imitate visually those often bizarre and fantastic images of one's "private vision, emotional state, or subjective responses to objective reality" (Cook 1996, 964). Cinema scholars would offer as examples Robert Wiene's *Das Kabinett des Dr.*

Caligari and Fritz Lang's *Metropolis*. Buildings in both of these films are angular rather than rectangular and the lighting is often *chiaroscuro*. Dondis (1973, 138) offers up the Byzantine and the Gothic architectural styles as examples, saying "expressionistic style is present when the artist or designer is seeking to evoke a maximum emotional response from the viewer." The communication strategies characteristic of Expressionism are: exaggeration, spontaneity, activeness, complexity, roundness, boldness, variation, distortion, irregularity, juxtaposition, and verticality. The elemental approach to the assessment of visual persuasion examines the basic components of images and the strategies employed in their use.

As mentioned above, this elemental approach to the assessment of visual persuasion has been used in examining architecture in general (Ragsdale 2011). Since it is fair to say that an examination of designed spaces is merely an extension of the elements of architectural design, a brief summary of the approach to the assessment of architecture should be helpful. Space is in fact one of the elements of architectural design. The basic principles of architectural design may first be found in written form in the ten books of Vitruvius (1960). While Vitruvius was explicit in explaining these basic principles, his list was rather general. Modern authors fortunately provide more elaborated lists. Strickland (2001, xi-xiv), for example, includes the following: rhythm, line, scale or size, light, texture, color, ornament, acoustics, site, space, weight/mass. Roth's (1993) list is not appreciably different from Strickland's. He lists: proportion, scale, rhythm, texture, light, color, ugliness, ornament, acoustics, space, function, and "firmeness." Roth's treatment of space is very appropriate for the assessments proposed in this book.

Ching (1973) is quite aware of the interaction of the basic elements of visual design with communication strategies as Dondis describes them in architectural design. He begins his account with the basic elements: points, lines, planes, and volume and then shows how form and space are organized according to the principles of circulation, proportion, and scale following a familiar set of principles: an axis, symmetry, hierarchy, rhythm/repetition, a datum, and transformation. While his list of principles is shorter than those of Strickland and Roth, Ching shows more explicitly than either of the other two writers how such elements of architecture as rhythm, line, and scale are related to the more fundamental basic elements and communication strategies.

Three examples from *Compelling Form* (Ragsdale 2011) should suffice to illustrate the elemental approach. First, there is the Gothic cathedral, which, among other significant design features, relies on rhythm, scale, light, and ornament. If one were to break down the power of the cathedral's overall effect into its components, these design features would stand out in explaining that power. Rhythm can be seen, for example in repeated arched windows, scale in the footprint of the cathedral and the height of the spires and towers, light in the clerestory and rose windows, and ornament in the exterior carvings at the entryways.

Second, many buildings are made compelling by their sites. The Louvre, for example, is not only centrally located in Paris but lies at the terminus of the grand avenue, the Champs Élysées. The Parthenon in Athens is on the hill of the Acropolis. The Colosseum in Rome is located adjacent to the Forum, and Durham Cathedral lies within the walls of Durham Castle at the top of a hill above a moat-like river. Third, some buildings are visually compelling because they are so perfectly symmetrical. Examples are easy to find in both Classical and Neoclassical architecture: the Roman Pantheon, the British Museum, and the Philadelphia Museum of Art. When one concludes that the use of these design features makes a building compelling or visually persuasive, he or she is relying on the knowledge of Gestalt psychology which explains how such features are perceived. The central concern of this book, however, is designed spaces, so it is appropriate next to consider space as one of the basic elements of architectural design.

"Space constantly encompasses our being. Through the volume of space, we move, see forms and objects, hear sounds, feel breezes, smell the fragrances of a flower garden in bloom. It is a material substance like wood or stone. Yet it is inherently formless. Its visual form, quality of light, dimensions and scale, depend totally on its boundaries as defined by elements of form" (Ching 1979, 108). It is easy to lose sight of the significance space plays in our lives, yet as soon as one is caught in a traffic jam or a seemingly endless queue at some event one becomes aware immediately that there is not enough space. In truth, one may need space almost as much psychologically as one needs water physiologically. As noted before, space is one of the elements of architecture, such that buildings cannot be properly assessed for their visual power without considering the spaces surrounding them and the spaces they enclose.

There are four kinds of space considered with regard to buildings. There is "purely *physical space*, which can be imagined as the volumes of air bounded by the walls, floor, and ceiling of a room" (Roth 1993, 45). Positive space would be the most obvious type of physical space, "one that is conceived as a void, then wrapped in the built shell erected to define and contain it." Within all buildings are positive physical spaces. Less obvious, and less common as well, is negative space, which is that "created by hollowing out a solid that already exists" (51). A cave is a negative space, as is a tunnel.

The second kind of space is *"Perceptual space"*—the space that can be perceived or seen. Especially in a building with walls of glass, this perceptual space may be extensive indeed and impossible to quantify" (Roth 1993, 45). Often, comparatively small houses rely on glass to give the impression of more space. Several art museums around the world use the same principle for dramatic effect in their foyers. The Christchurch Art Gallery in New Zealand comes immediately to mind, along with the Metropolitan Museum of Art and the Museum of Modern Art in Manhattan. Standing in the foyer of the Christchurch museum and looking out suggests a vista including the area outside the building. The rotunda dome at the Met draws one's eyes to the sky outside.

"Related to perceptual space is **conceptual space,** which can be defined as the mental map we carry around in our heads, the plan stored in our memory" (Roth 1993, 45). Many art museums consist of galleries of loosely connected rooms. Although galleries are usually numbered so that one may experience a collection in some sensible order, the memory one has afterward may be more of a maze or a rabbit warren.

Finally, "the architect also decisively shapes **behavioral space,** or the space we can actually move through and use" (Roth 1993, 45). Behavioral space may be, and most often is, directional. Roth points out that in the Gothic cathedral there is only one path, and that is the one which leads to the altar. Shopping malls most often use directional space to insure that customers are drawn to certain stores. Casinos are arranged directionally to lead visitors to the gambling venues that are the most popular or that have the greatest potential for the house. Less often, one encounters nondirectional space, where many paths lead to the same end point. Zoos especially, but also parks and gardens, exemplify nondirectional space. However, pathways in zoos, parks, and gardens are often laid out to direct visitors to highly popular venues within.

As Roth (1993, 49) points out "with slight redefining, these terms can be used to describe experiences in large outdoor spaces as well," so the term designed spaces is an inclusive one and ranges from the interiors of such monumental structures as the Pantheon in Rome, Salisbury Cathedral in the UK, and Versailles to the exterior designed spaces of flower beds and lawns of a personal residence to the vast parks and hunting preserves of European kings. The emphasis in this book is on exterior designed spaces, thus exterior spaces are the starting point. Following the assessment of exteriors, however, the book will also consider several interior spaces in order to assess the element of space in significant buildings more thoroughly than in previous works (e.g., Ragsdale 2011). Since shopping malls illustrate directional space especially well, they will also be included.

In this volume, the exterior designed spaces which will be examined include parks and gardens, national parks, zoological gardens and parks, amusement parks, battlefield memorials, and national cemeteries. In examining these designed spaces as visual persuasion, the typical approach will be the elemental one, with semiotic analysis when it is called for by the particular space. Next, however, a fundamentally important issue must be addressed. This issue is the nature of the response to a visually persuasive stimulus. As reported earlier, visual images may be used as supporting materials for a verbal proposition, and in this way they function just like facts, statistics, and examples do in verbal persuasion. It is not clear, however, just what the response is to a visual image standing on its own and the extent to which that response can legitimately be called a persuasive one.

The central outcomes of verbal persuasion are attitude change and behavior change. As noted previously, little consideration has been given to the outcomes of visual persuasion when it is an image standing alone that is the stimulus. In a previous work (Ragsdale 2011), the effects of standalone images were said to be compelling, a term presumably synonymous with attitude or behavior change. To date, the precise meaning of the term compelling has not been rigorously addressed. The reason for this oversight, if you will, is that it is almost self-evident that an image has some effect on the viewer. Think about the contemplation of a Gothic cathedral, a painting such as *La joconde*, a Robert Capa photograph, or a museum building such as the Guggenheim in Manhattan. It would seem hard to imagine a person not being affected by such images. However, it is equally hard to describe just what that effect is.

One would like to think that the images mentioned above are simply beautiful and that beauty, in turn, is persuasive, meaning that beauty is a mediating variable in the process of visual persuasion. There are two immediate problems with this explanation however. The first is that beauty itself is not a term or a response with which everyone agrees. Through the centuries, that which constitutes beauty has varied as well (Eco 2004). The second and more serious problem is that the aesthetic response which beauty evokes may not necessarily be persuasive. As if these two problems were not enough, there is also the lack of any carefully described connection between an aesthetic response and either attitude or behavior change. Ultimately also, there are issues to consider such as whether or not an image that is not beautiful is persuasive and what the visual effect is of an image which is outright ugly. The first step would seem to be an analysis of just what a persuasive response is. If the simplest response to persuasion is attitude change, then an examination of the nature of an attitude is the proper beginning point.

In the middle of the 20th century, the psychologist Charles Osgood and his associates developed a measuring instrument called the semantic differential (Osgood, Suci, and Tannenbaum 1957). Although initially intended to explore the nature of meaning, the semantic differential came to be widely used to measure a large variety of psychological and linguistic variables including attitude. The instrument is a simple list of bipolar adjectives separated by seven-point scales used to measure the closeness of a test taker's response to one end or the other of the scale and with respect to a particular word, behavior, or concept such as cigarette smoking. It turns out that the adjectives represent the underlying dimensions of the connotative meaning of, say, cigarette smoking. Not all bipolar pairs go together, which is to say that connotative meaning is a multidimensional concept. "Good" and "bad," for example, measure the same thing as "positive" and "negative." However, "hot" and "cold" and "strong" and "weak" are not in the same semantic universe.

Interestingly, one factor emerged as a recurring element of meaning as well as the factor accounting for most of the error variance in each case. That factor was labeled the evaluative factor, since it was characterized by such bipolar adjective pairs as "good" and "bad." In simple terms, the research of Osgood and associates showed that virtually all responses on the semantic differential included a large amount of evaluation. We either like things or we don't. How, then, is this finding related to our concern with the nature of an attitude? The answer turns out to be quite simple: an attitude is itself a predisposition to react to something in a positive or negative way (Gass and Seiter 2014). Humans seem to have attitudes about everything!

It is necessary, then, to describe part of the response to an isolated visual image, i.e., one that is not obviously being used as a warrant to support a claim, as an evaluative one. We may well see a cathedral such as Notre-Dame de Paris as evidence of the power of the Church, but we do not have to do so to respond to it as a persuasive message. Its design elements alone affect our attitudes. These effects may not be the same for each viewer. Some may not find a view of Notre-Dame to be negative rather than positive, but the result of the viewing is an attitudinal one nonetheless. This view suggests that the attitudinal response is not necessarily one mediated by the aesthetic one. The two responses may be separate or overlapping, and one may indeed mediate the other for some viewers. Moreover, there would clearly be an attitudinal component to human responses to ugly or repulsive visual images, although the nature of the attitude would be quite the opposite of one's attitude toward a beautiful image. For this reason, the term "compelling" would seem to continue to be an appropriate adjective to describe the effects of visual images.

It is much more difficult to assess any behavioral effects of compelling visual images, but this is true of assessing behavioral effects of traditional persuasion. We know, for example, that there is no one-to-one relationship between attitude change and behavior change (Gass and Seiter 2014). While it would be comforting to think that presenting a convincing case for attitude change would result in behavior change, we know that this is too often not the case. Most cigarette smokers, for example and regrettably, know that their smoking may lead to a variety of cancers, heart disease, and breathing difficulties, yet they continue to smoke. The truth is that behavior change involves more variables than just one's attitudes. Among these are social norms and behavioral intentions. Research at this stage does not indicate what behavioral changes might be associated with viewing isolated visual images, such as cathedrals, skyscrapers, or public gardens, but we do know that visual experiences inform future such experiences, much like the notion of standards of taste, so that behavior probably is altered over time. Whatever the case, there seems little reason to doubt the power of visual images to persuade, even when these images stand alone. In the following chapter, the central focus is on what are perhaps the most typical kinds of designed spaces to be examined in this book: gardens and parks.

CHAPTER TWO

BEYOND BUILDINGS:
PLEASURE GARDENS AND PARKS

"No doubt about it. The first gardens were not made, but discovered. A natural spot—a clearing in the forest, a valley opening up in a barren mountain-side, an island in a remote lake—made pleasant by a belt of trees, flowering, fragrant, and bearing fruit. . . . In the oldest accounts, such spots are the gardens of the gods, or of those favoured by the gods" (Thacker 1979, 9). Even today, the idea of such a "sacred grove" clearly lies at the heart of the US national park system, where natural spots are set apart and preserved for all to see. However, humans appear also to have thought of creating gardens from the earliest times and for a variety of reasons, such as raising food—vegetables, grains, fruits, and nuts. In this chapter, the focus will be on the pleasure garden, since it is this kind of spot where one may most clearly see the deliberate use of elements of visual design for persuasive effect.

There were, of course, a variety of reasons for building pleasure gardens. Stuart (2010) identifies four. One reason was to provide a place for spiritual retreat or as simply a place to escape from stress. "The garden at Stourhead in England was intended to transport the visitor into a higher realm; its idealized landscape recalls to our minds the backgrounds in Claude Lorrain's classical paintings, and the virtues of ancient Rome, or, perhaps more accurately, Whig interpretations of the classical world" (17). A second reason was to provide a pleasing outdoor space in which to socialize. The great public gardens of France, like Paris's Jardin du Luxembourg, exemplify such spaces as do the walled gardens within European castles. The gardens within Prague castle illustrate this latter type. Even in such modest examples as the backyards of today's private residences, one can see the desire for a place to socialize.

Stuart's (2010) third motive specifically identifies pleasure gardens as means of visual persuasion. "A third universal motive for making a garden is far from spiritual or social: it is to impress others with one's wealth and power—power over others and power over nature" (19). The prime example in the world is Louis XIV's Versailles. It "is one of the most deliberate statements of power that it is possible to find in garden history; the straight lines cut through woodland and the central avenue that had no ending proclaimed to the assembled French nobility, and to the world,

Louis' complete self-confidence and his enormous ambition" (20-21). Again, in such modest circumstances as the modern American suburban home, one can see evidence of homeowners wanting "to outdo their neighbours in splendor and display" (21).

Stuart's final reason for building pleasure gardens is no less significant in our understanding of them as means of visual persuasion than the previous motive. "A fourth universal motive for making a pleasure garden, rather than a garden in which to produce food to eat, is the human desire to create beautiful patterns, to order our environment, to create works of art that express something of the aesthetic taste and the personality of their creator" (2010, 21). As has been evident in previous studies of buildings (e.g., Ragsdale 2011), it is these very "beautiful patterns" resulting from the deliberate application of the basic elements of visual design that evoke the aesthetic response that may be regarded as the outcome of visual persuasion. In what follows, some of the most powerfully expressive of the world's pleasure gardens will be considered as means of visual persuasion. This consideration will assess the underlying means by which these gardens produce these effects. To facilitate these assessments, some essential principles of general landscape design will be considered first.

"Landscape design is the art and science of organizing and enriching outdoor space through the placement of plants and structures in agreeable and useful relationships with the natural environment" (Van Der Zanden and Rodie 2008, 107). Not surprisingly, the essential principles of landscape design do not differ appreciably than those already introduced in this book having to do with general design principles. Compared to the design of a building, however, there are several important differences. One is that the site of the landscape is ordinarily a given. There is a particular lot or location which defines the space to be designed, and in most cases this space may not only have irregular boundaries but may not conform to a particular geometric shape. A building, by contrast, is located in a space and not defined by it for the most part. In the case of some pleasure gardens, however, the space is manipulated as part of the design. Versailles is a notable example.

Another difference between landscape design and architectural design is that growing plants and grasses, pools and streams, and rock formations must be accommodated in the plan. The location of such items may not be conducive to a compelling view and may have to be relocated or have their appearances changed. A third difference is that a landscape, as opposed to a building, is a growing entity, which must be continually and regularly tended so as to preserve the design. However, the visual appearance of a garden is no different than any other thing in its impact, which is to say that at its base the garden is a composite of basic elements of design.

"Human engagement and understanding of the landscape are significantly enhanced when four characteristics are evident," say Van Der Zanden and Rodie (2008, 124). These are coherence, complexity, legibility, and mystery. Coherence refers to logical and understandable divisions. Complexity refers to "a balance of texture, color, form, and size variety." Legibility and mystery are less obvious in their meanings. Legibility means that the landscape is "readable," so that the visitor will not fear becoming lost. Mystery refers to unusual design features "or the promise of something just around the corner." Ultimately, these four characteristics are the products of such familiar basic elements as line, form, color, texture, and space, especially positive and negative spaces.

Having identified these characteristics and mentioned again familiar basic elements, there is a need to enumerate the most common ingredients of landscaping, many of which will be familiar to the reader. Perhaps the most obvious ingredient in a garden is its **avenues**. These pathways vary from the broad avenues of a large garden or park such as Versailles to the narrow and sometimes twisting pathways of a much more modest garden. Avenues serve two functions. One function may be to call attention to the immensity of the landscape, to draw the eye toward the horizon and emphasize the horizontal dimension of space. Another function is revelatory. Avenues insure that the visitor follows the direction that insures he or she sees everything and sees it in the planned order.

Pools or ponds and reflecting pools provide an element of nature that is essential to pleasure gardens. "People restore themselves mentally and physically in natural settings. Natural views and access to the outdoors have been shown to enhance healing in hospitals, reduce neighborhood violence, reduce blood pressure and stress, and improve accuracy in simple task completion" (Van Der Zanden and Rodie 2008, 127). Water is, of course, essential to natural settings. **Fountains** are another essential ingredient of the pleasure garden.

Of course, gardens would not be gardens without **plants and lawns**. These range from a multitude of flowering plants to shrubs and hedges to varieties of trees. Flowering plants provide the element of color as well as fragrance. Hedges delineate sections of a garden, line avenues, and stand alone. Standalone hedges may be intricately sculpted into topiaries used especially for ornamentation. Hedges delineate **parterres**, which are individual geometrical plots within the overall landscape often containing formal plantings. A particular type of parterre is the **knot garden**, which is most often a square whose plantings within follow a design such as a chain link or a knot. What follows now is an assessment of a variety of representative pleasure gardens in terms of our understanding of space and of basic landscape design elements and ingredients.

The Gardens of Italy: The Source of Modern Pleasure Garden Design

"In the making of pleasure gardens, as in so many other arts, the Italians taught the whole of Europe a lesson, and set the standards by which civilized gardens were to be judged" (Stuart 2010, 119). There were and there remain today many fine examples of the Italian pleasure garden, so that the traveler may find a notable site almost wherever he or she alights. The discussion here will focus on three of these: the Boboli Gardens in Florence, the Villa d'Este in Tivoli, and the Villa Lante at Bagnaia. The Villa Borghese Gardens in Rome are also significant for this account, but this site is unlike the other three. It is a large city park and will be considered in the following chapter. These examples provide a representative sample of the Italian visual style. Of course, the cultural history of these villas and their gardens is a compelling study in its own right, and there are ample sources available for the reader to pursue and which also are vividly illustrated with photographs and drawings.

One of the architectural wonders of Florence is the Palazzo Pitti, but the Boboli Gardens behind the building are perhaps even more spectacular. Directly behind the palace, the gardens lie within a horseshoe shaped landscape. A central avenue divides this part of the garden symmetrically. Smaller avenues crisscross the garden to allow access to parterres on the west side of the lower horseshoe. There is both a lower and an upper amphitheatre populated by trees and hedges which follow the line of the horseshoe shape. If defined only by the limits of the palace itself, the gardens would roughly form a triangle, but the gardens have been extended eastward to form a much more vast collection of parterres divided by another central avenue lined by cypress trees. Near the end of this avenue is an oval pond in which there is an oval island with a fountain statue of Oceanus. Statuary is interspersed throughout the garden.

So what is the visual persuasive power of the Boboli Gardens? Its trees and hedges give a sense of a natural setting, and its layout is symmetrical just behind the Palazzo Pitti and then again when one takes the avenue leading to the eastern edge. While there is complexity in this large space, there is no loss of coherence. The water adds to the natural setting. The overall impression one has of the Boboli Gardens is that of harmony

Fig. 2-1 Boboli Gardens

within a formal set of design parameters. Line, geometric shape, and directional space underlie this harmony making these gardens a popular tourist destination.

Due east of Rome, Tivoli is home to the Villa d'Este and its elaborate garden emphasizing a variety of water effects. Built by Cardinal Ippolito d'Este, governor of Tivoli, this garden lies on a hillside leading up to the villa and consists of a series of terraces (Boults and Sullivan 2010). The main avenue to the villa is crossed horizontally by other avenues leading to large parterres and fish ponds. To the left, before one ascends from the lowest part of the garden, is the huge Organ Fountain, which distributed water to the garden and was able to produce trumpet sounds (Boults and Sullivan 2010). At the top of the next major terrace is the crisscrossing Avenue of the 100 Fountains, where narrow walled terraces feature stonework figures spraying water forward and upward. Just in front of this avenue is a single fountain, the Oval Fountain.

The hedges, trees, and lawn of the d'Este garden are the main source of color, which is green, along with the blue water of the various fountains and ponds. The garden also has numerous sculptures interspersed throughout its area, many of which came from Hadrian's villa in Tivoli. The garden of the Villa d'Este, like the Boboli Gardens, has a symmetrical

Fig. 2-2 Villa d'Este

layout of cross-axes providing a harmonious visual impact. Its design parameters are formal ones dependent on line, geometry, and directional space. The Villa d'Este is more compact and less diverse than the Boboli Gardens, but the combination of water, fountains, and greenery give the visitor the impression of serenity in a natural setting.

Home of Cardinal Gianfrancesco Gambara, the Villa Lante at Bagnaia features a compact and perfectly symmetrical garden built on the edge of a large forest to the north and east. Like Villa d'Este, the Villa Lante centers around greenery and water as well as a slope from the villa downward. At the lowest point of the slope is a large pool divided into four parterres with a huge fountain at its center. Surrounding the fountain are parterres of carefully sculpted hedges in geometric forms. Each has a central point with spokes radiating outward. Like the Villa d'Este, the Villa Lante is a composition in greenery, water, and statuary. "The essential elements of the Italian garden—light and shade, terraces descending a steep hillside, water moving and still, sculpture, elegant pavilions, balustrades and steps—work together in a modest, unceremonious way. The absolute symmetry of the layout, with the fountains marking the central axis, gives a feeling of repose" (Stuart 2010, 131).

Fig. 2-3 Villa Lante

Noting terms such as "serenity" and "repose," it is clear that the mood or reaction of the visitor to such gardens as the ones presented here is part of what might legitimately be called visual persuasion. Largely aesthetic in its essence, the reaction was one undoubtedly intended by the original designers and builders. These Italian gardens permitted celebrations, weddings, polite socializing, and simple contemplation, among other things, and afforded their owners an opportunity to assert their financial and aesthetic superiority in the areas around them. As noted, Italian gardens greatly influenced the design of gardens in Europe generally. While the influence of these garden designs can be seen in those of France and England, nothing quite compares to the scale of the French and later the English designs. Additionally, the formality of the French gardens was much more extreme than that of the Italian.

The Gardens of France

"In 17th-century France, people's attitudes toward nature changed. Nature was not considered beautiful until human order was imposed upon it. Shrubs were clipped into hedges, trees trimmed to form *palissades*, contours graded with precision, rivers diverted, lands inscribed with straight paths and *allées,* and the ground decorated with *parterres de*

Fig. 2-4 Vaux le Vicomte

broderie" (Boults and Sullivan 2010, 136). As a result, two design features set French pleasure gardens apart from virtually all others in Europe.

One design feature was scale, which was vast, while the other was the geometric design precision which extended all the way from the general layout of the garden to the programmatic and severe shaping of the parterres and hedges. "A spatial dynamic developed based on breakthroughs in physics and mathematics. The mathematics of infinity as developed by René Descartes implied 'limitless' space" (Boults and Sullivan 2010, 136). The influence of this idea resulted in long, wide avenues extending as far as the eye could see. Breathtaking in their scope, these avenues employed what is essentially a very basic visual element: a straight line extended into apparent infinity.

As he or she traveled along this long and broad vista—there was usually only one main one—the visitor could take pleasure in statuary, pools, and fountains along the way, especially at Versailles where compelling statuary was used as the basis of fountains within pools. Additionally, one would encounter rigidly trimmed shrubs in such forms as cones or balls or topiaries. In the graveled areas near the palace in Versailles, one would find baskets of orange trees which could be rolled into a greenhouse when the weather became too cold for them to thrive outside. Finally, the visitor would encounter the characteristic parterre de broderie, which could be seen in Italy but which was taken to a higher level in France. These parterres were squares outlined with square box hedges within which were plantings whose sculpted shapes represented coats of arms, figures, and geometric designs as if they were embroidered. This account of the formal French garden includes the gardens at Vaux le Vicomte and at Versailles.

Designed by the landscape architect André le Nôtre, the interior designer Charles le Brun, who was le Nôtre's fellow student and friend, and the architect Louis II le Vau, the chateau and gardens at Vaux le Vicomte were built for the finance minister of Louis XIV, Nicolas Fouquet (Steenbergen and Reh 2003). The project was so vast that it required the razing of three entire villages and used more than 18,000 workers (Boults and Sullivan 2010). Le Nôtre was the son of the man in charge of the Tuileries Gardens of the Louvre in Paris. As a young man, he not only studied landscape design but a number of other disciplines which he was able to bring to bear on his later work: geometry, architecture, and painting. "Le Notre (*sic*) understood space as an abstraction, and was able to impart more clarity and unity on the style of his predecessors. His was an ordered geometry based on Cartesian logic" (137).

Although Versailles was much larger, Vaux le Vicomte may well be the quintessential French formal garden. The approach to the chateau was through the forest, which opens up to a hemispheric parking area fronting the chateau grounds. In front of the chateau, there is an avenue leading to a fence and entry gate. Flanking the avenue, both before and after passing through the gate, are large parterres of grass behind which are several outbuildings. On either side of the chateau, the pattern of lawn set off as rectangular parterres continues to the rear, where the avenue passes between parterres de broderie and shrubs shaped into cones and balls. An oval fountain lies in the middle of the avenue, followed by circular ponds to either side. The avenue ends at a low colonnaded rampart denoting a rise in the land, but the vista continues beyond in the form of a broad, grassy avenue leading to the horizon and surrounded by woods (Steenbergen and Reh 2003). It is just the sort of garden one would have predicted that Le Nôtre would design.

The size of Vaux le Vicomte's gardens is powerfully compelling as evidence of great wealth. Louis was so impressed by it—probably even jealous of it—that he had Fouquet imprisoned on the grounds of financial impropriety and confiscated plants and other feature of Vaux for use at Versailles. In this case, Fouquet's effort at visual persuasion was singularly unproductive. And Louis also commissioned le Nôtre to design and build the gardens of Versailles. Apart from the political considerations, the garden itself is a testament to the sensibility of the age, wherein geometric patterns, Cartesian space, grand vistas, and formal

Fig. 2-5 Versailles

shapes and patterns were undoubtedly quite compelling visually. Even today, a much less formally oriented period, the garden is visually compelling for its proportion, symmetry, and use of such basic elements as line and shape.

Versailles, which the three builders of Vaux were hired to create, was of course the most extravagant and extensive palace and grounds ever built and which was to influence countless later European imitators. The land itself is heavily forested and had previously been a royal hunting ground. Much of the forest to the rear of the palace remains today, the gardens having been quite literally carved out of the woods. Versailles is clearly a le Nôtre design and highly reminiscent of Vaux le Vicomte. In scope, the gardens at Versailles are impossible to describe in complete detail given the scope of this book, therefore the most significant parts will be the focus here.

The approach to Versailles today is from the city of Versailles some 15 miles southeast of Paris. The entrance is through a black iron gate with golden finials and upward over a huge paved courtyard presided over by a large statue of the Sun King astride his horse. The main palace spreads horizontally parallel to the entry gate with two wings stretching toward the gate on either side of the courtyard. The gardens begin behind the palace.

The palace sits on a gentle slope so that the gardens extend down and away, ultimately to the horizon. Aside from being larger than Vaux, Versailles is distinguished primarily from its predecessor by the Grand Canal which forms a large section of the broad avenue leading away from the palace and a large number of fountains featuring bronze sculptures such as the Bassin d'Apollon.

Other smaller avenues run parallel to the central one making the gardens of Versailles broader also than the one at Vaux. Each of the avenues is flanked by shrubs sculpted into cones and balls, abundant statuary, parterres with diagonal patterns, and parterres de broderie. The greenery and the water are the dominant themes of the gardens. "Parties, banquets, ballets—all kinds of events and spectacles were staged in the *bosquets*, the garden rooms carved out of the ornamental groves in different geometric patterns" (Boults and Sullivan 2010, 141-142). There is little doubt that Louis XIV wanted his palace and its grounds to be unequalled in the world. Not only were they to be visually compelling—a testament to the Sun King himself—there were to be the places where his court and his visitors could experience pleasures and sights equal to no other.

Today's visitor as well as those of Louis' time would have great difficulty experiencing the entirety of Versailles without the many minibuses which ply the avenues of the grounds. "Although organized around a central axis like Vaux-le-Vicomte, the gardens at Versailles were so large and the attractions so numerous that no clear logic existed to visually lead one through the space" (Boults and Sullivan 2010, 143). As Louis aged and the visitors and spectacles diminished, the King wandered in his gardens for the simple pleasures they afforded him and actually wrote a book and many revisions which was an itinerary for the visitor. Across the Channel, the English carried on the principles of pleasure gardening perhaps first encountered in Renaissance Italy but, like the French, transformed those principles into distinctly British versions of the pleasure garden.

English Landscape Gardens and Flower Gardens

"In the 17th century, English gardens were a mix of French and Dutch styles adapted to different environmental circumstances. In the 18th century, those foreign, formal styles were overthrown in favor of a more English, 'natural' style. Landscape gardens, as they came to be called, were equally as contrived as formal gardens, but somehow people

Fig. 2-6 Castle Howard

interpreted irregular geometries as being more representative of nature than straight lines" (Boults and Sullivan 2010, 151). The emergence of these landscape gardens was influenced to a large degree by politics, specifically anti-French and anti-Roman Catholic sentiment. Even poets and philosophers of the time advocated a "freer style of landscape design" and promoted the idea of nature as its basis.

At the same time, Parliament passed the Enclosure Acts, which were intended to promote agriculture but which primarily caused large parcels of land to be moved from public to private ownership. The landed gentry subsequently enclosed large portions of their estates and termed them parks. In addition to the production of timber and their use as grazing land for cattle, these parks were used much as pleasure gardens had been used before. What strikes one as most distinctive of these landscape gardens is how expansive they were. They were also often devoid of the geometric designs, parterres, and sculpted shrubs of either the Italian or the French gardens. In their place was gently rolling open countryside, sprinkled with trees in their natural state and divided by streams and pools. In addition, pavilions and statues were placed irregularly throughout these gardens. Three examples of the English landscape garden are to be found at Castle Howard, at Stowe, and at Stourhead. They are not unlike many of the large city parks to be found today in many parts of the Western world and which will be assessed in the next chapter.

Castle Howard was the palatial residence of Charles Howard, Lord Carlisle located a short distance northeast of York near the British border with Scotland (Steenbergen and Reh 2003). The approach to the castle was similar to the approach to Vaux le Vicomte and is the only part of the

Fig. 2-7 Stowe

castle's gardens that bears much resemblance to older landscape designs. Three avenues bordered by lawn and trees enclose parterres, although these enclosures contain primarily open lawns. The central avenue is bisected by a horizontal avenue in the middle of which is a circular fountain. Trimmed hedges border the parterres. Beyond the castle, the gardens open up into a striking example of the English landscape garden. A vast lawn, wider than the castle and its outbuildings, slopes gently down to a huge manmade lake lined with trees, which stretches outward in a pattern roughly like that of a boot. The expanse, although manmade, has the rough hewn look of a natural piece of land.

"In terms of landscape architecture, Stowe [in Buckinghamshire] is England's most complex landscape garden and is probably the best example of the 18th-century experimental tradition. . . . Between 1713 and 1780 three successive generations of owners, together with their architects and artists, created a picturesque landscape which. . . . is the *locus classicus* of picturesque landscape architecture" (Steenbergen and Reh 2003, 291). The land belonged to the Temple family in the 16th century, of which Viscount Cobham founded the palace at Stowe. A succession of Temple family members worked on the grounds through the end of the 18th century. Like the garden at Castle Howard, Stowe is vast and replete with rolling lawns bordered by groves of trees, a lake and streams, and is intermingled with statues, arches, and a Gothic temple. The northern approach to the palace is a triangular space of two lawn parterres through which runs a single avenue leading to the house. Before this is a wide and deep lawn planted so that it has alternating shades of green rows and columns suggesting a checkerboard. The parterres are planted in this fashion as well.

Fig. 2-8 Stourhead

Behind the house, as at Castle Howard, there is an immense lawn at Stowe planted with the checkerboard lawn which gives way to a plain lawn at the end of which is the lake. Beyond the lake the land opens up into the rolling lawn bordered by trees, but the estate is so vast that roads have had to be built within to permit one to see the whole—nearly 900 acres (Boults and Sullivan 2010). Numerous structures were added to the garden in addition to the Gothic temple mentioned above. Some had political or philosophical virtues associated with them and included a Temple of Ancient Virtue, a Temple of British Worthies, a Palladian Bridge, and a Temple of Concord and Virtue.

At Stourhead in Wiltshire, the landscape garden also has a theme, but this one is a Classical literary one. A "path leads the visitor in a counterclockwise direction, relating a sequence of events from Virgil's *The Aeneid*—the story of the voyage to Rome by Aeneas and the Trojan survivors. From the Temple of Apollo, the ultimate stop on the itinerary, the whole garden becomes visible" (Boults and Sullivan 2010, 159).

Stourhead was begun in 1735 by its owner Henry Hoare II who built the landscape garden in a small valley around a 20 acre lake which was manmade. The path mentioned above is a circular walk around the lake. Although Stourhead House was no less imposing than Castle Howard and the palace at Stowe, the landscape garden is much smaller and more intimate than either of the preceding gardens.

If one is to understand what is visually compelling about these English landscape gardens, it will be necessary to have some idea of the 18th century idea of nature. Alexander Pope, one of the most prominent chroniclers of the Age of Enlightenment, as the 18th century is called, wrote: "Nature and Nature's laws lay hid in night. God said 'Let Newton be,' and all was light." This proposed epitaph for Newton, at once, captures not only the veneration in which the man was held during his life but something of the essence of the 18th century. The Age of Enlightenment set aside the teachings of the church and of clerics in matters of all kinds in favor of scientific investigation. Investigation of what? Why, nature of course.

The century is rife with examples of learned men seeking answers to everything from science to art by observing the natural world. It was thought that nature was itself orderly and contained the answers to all questions that might previously have been referred to a cleric. The natural world, as the source of answers to questions about science and art took on an air of an entity to be admired or even worshipped and as the standard by which judgments should be made. Art, for example, was thought of by some to take place by holding a mirror up to nature. For others, art was nature improved upon, presumably to remove some of nature's wildness. How appropriate, then, that the idea of a landscape garden should be something that looked like nature, albeit improved upon by manmade artifice (Cassirer 1955).

Why were these landscape gardens visually persuasive? Their basic elements, like those of great examples of architecture, were not numerous. Scale, of course, was probably the most significant element in their compelling effect. Color, albeit primarily green, was another important element. These gardens were simple, which is a reflection of the British denigration of the formal—and Catholic—French garden, and they reflected economy as opposed to intricacy. Viewed from a distance or from above, English landscape gardens were not symmetrical or balanced in a Classical sense but most were designed with paths and avenues leading the visitor through them in reasonable sequentiality. These visual elements, added to the sense that being out in the natural world was almost like worship, made for a most compelling effect on the visitor.

Fig. 2-9 East Ruston Old Vicarage

English garden has another meaning which is quite different from that portrayed to this point, and it is the idea of a flower garden, a small space attached to a house in which were planted a profusion of flowering plants. This almost unique British creation was the product of many influences. As the British Empire expanded, sailors brought home plants from many exotic places, "but even before the days of Empire the English were fascinated with a wide variety of plants" (Stuart 2010, 189). The Romans brought flowers to England, and the cultivation of flowers became popular with churchmen. Herbs became popular to plant for medicinal purposes, and the word "florist" appeared first in the English language in the 17th century.

Two specific reasons for the rise of the English flower garden, however, were the rise of the middle class, which lacked the personal funds and aristocratic titles for large landscape gardens, and the comparatively smaller building lots and residential spaces of the urban areas in which many members of the middle class lived. Of course, England is "a well-watered, maritime environment with few excesses of heat or cold. Gardening is therefore easier in Great Britain than in many other parts of the world" (Stuart 2010, 189). Whatever the reasons, Britons are flower gardeners. "In the United Kingdom there are 3,500 gardens open under the National Gardens Scheme." Moreover, books and pamphlets on gardening have been ubiquitous throughout the realm quite literally for centuries.

Fig. 2-10 Biddulph Grange

It is much less easy to characterize a flower garden than any other garden assessed in this chapter previously. For one thing, these gardens are both smaller and consequently more numerous than their larger varieties. Because of their primary association with private residences, English flower gardens are rather harder to identify, although to be sure there are a number for which illustrative photographs are available. Perhaps the most obvious characteristic of flower gardens is a profusion of color. Reds, blues, lavenders, yellows, whites, and virtually every other color imaginable may be found in a single garden. Different shades of green augment and provide a background for the colors of blossoms. Obviously, fragrances fill the air, providing an olfactory reinforcement to the varying visual stimuli.

Fig. 2-11 Hidcote Manor

These gardens are smaller than the English landscape garden, but this is not to say that all of them are tiny. At some church related properties, such as East Ruston Old Vicarage, and at some large residences, such as Biddulph Grange and Hidcote Manor, these flower gardens may be quite large compared to those at urban residences. Small, meandering paths and small ponds and streams are reminiscent of the larger Italian pleasure gardens. Planting is usually in beds, and these can range from long, rectangular areas abutting fences to smaller freestanding beds formed in circles, triangles, and squares. English flower gardens give pleasure to their owners and visitors, provide a place to socialize, and are visually compelling for their evocation of natural settings. From the tradition of the English landscape garden, as well as the English inclination toward flower gardening, gardens have emerged on a national scale which intend to cultivate, feature, and promote all of the native plants of the realm. These royal or in some cases national botanical gardens are vast, like landscape gardens, but are also full of varieties of flowers and other plants, so that a visit to one of them is quite similar to a visit to any of the ones which have been discussed in this section of the chapter.

The Royal Botanical Gardens at Kew, Sydney, and Melbourne, and the Botanic Gardens at Wellington and Christchurch

The Royal Botanical Gardens at Kew, near London, is the home of the

Fig. 2-12 Kew

world's largest collection of plants. Created in 1759, it covers 300 acres on the south bank of the Thames River and contains six glasshouses, a library, a museum, a herbarium, and a seedbank in addition to some 30,000 different types of plants. It is not only a prime tourist destination in England but is also a working scientific laboratory and training center for horticulturists. As suggested above, Kew, as a garden, is a blend of the English landscape garden and the flower garden. While it is a national site, as opposed to an aristocratic or private one, there is little about its visual persuasiveness that is different from the other gardens discussed here.

Kew had been begun privately by Frederick, Prince of Wales, and his wife Augusta and was later developed extensively by Sir Joseph Banks. Banks was a wealthy amateur horticulturist who had traveled with Captain Cook in the south Pacific and collected plant specimens (Quest-Ritson 2003). The property abuts the Thames, as noted, and spreads out roughly in a rectangle interlaced with avenues and two lakes. Today, one can walk along an elevated avenue to see the gardens at treetop level. Kew is, if anything, a landscape park. It is interspersed with glasshouses and clusters of flowerbeds. There are exotic plants, such as rubber trees and palm trees, as well as miniature orchids and water lilies. A visit to Kew is visually compelling in its site along the River Thames and its profusion of colors. It is vast in scale and thus an icon of the city of London.

Fig. 2-13 Sydney Royal Botanic Gardens

The establishment of Kew led to royal or national botanical gardens in other locations in the UK, including Sydney and Melbourne, Australia, and Wellington and Christchurch, New Zealand. Sydney and Christchurch are similar in that they are primarily English landscape gardens featuring trees, especially trees indigenous to and unique to their respective countries. Like Kew, these botanical gardens are also research laboratories and preservation facilities. Perhaps the most famous site in Sydney is the Opera House. This is deservedly so, since there is no other building in the world quite like it visually. The Opera House sits on an outcropping of land on Circular Quay across from the Sydney Harbor Bridge. Just behind the Opera House spreading over 75 acres are the Sydney Royal Botanic Gardens, which form a U shape extending into the harbor and continuing back into the city to abut The Domain. The Domain was once the Governor's private landscape garden and is now a city park.

As with other landscape gardens, the Sydney Royal Botanic Gardens are interspersed with fountains and statuary, but they are most notable for their numerous trees. There are also stands of bamboo, many cacti, and multiple palm trees. There is an herb garden, and although this is primarily a landscape garden, there are many plots of flowering shrubs and plants. Although not directly pertinent to the concern for visual persuasion here, the gardens are also home to such a variety of birds that they are also a popular birding location.

The Sydney Royal Botanic Gardens are most compelling visually. They take advantage of an uncommon site bordering Sydney Harbor on one side and downtown Sydney on the other. The landscape follows gently rolling hills which suggest great freedom and openness. Color and the ornamentation provided by the plantings make a visit to the gardens a relaxing and peaceful event. The presence of such a space in this large city is an icon of the city's prestige and wealth, no less than the more famous Opera House.

Melbourne, south and west of Sydney along the coast, boasts several especially large landscape parks. An especially impressive one of these is the King's Domain, lying south of the city center off St. Kilda Road. The Royal Botanic Gardens adjoin this park and feature the large Ornamental Lake, a variety of different types of grassy lawns, such as the Tennyson Lawn, the Princes Lawn, and the Australian Lawn, an arid garden, and the National Herbarium. Like Kew on the Thames, the Melbourne gardens lie on the south bank of the Yarra River.

Across the ditch, as the Kiwis call the Tasman Sea between New Zealand and Australia, lies Wellington, the capital of New Zealand on the southernmost point of the North Island. New Zealand is a particularly fertile and green set of islands surrounded on all sides by ocean and characterized on land by the mountains that show their volcanic origin. Wellington, for example, is a harbor city, but one that almost immediately rises upward as one moves inland. At the peak of the hill overlooking Wellington, and connected to the city by a cable car, is the Wellington Botanic Garden. Hilly and forested, this botanic garden is quite a contrast to the more open one in Sydney. Like most botanic gardens, there are separate gardens within the park devoted to conifers, tulips, roses, and other specialized plantings. Also located in the park is the Carter Observatory. The area near the observatory gives spectacular views of the entire city of Wellington.

Fig. 2-14 Christchurch Botanic Gardens

Christchurch, on New Zealand's South Island, is sometimes called the country's Garden City, attributable in no small measure to the city's botanic gardens founded in 1863 with the planting of an English oak tree. The gardens occupy 52 acres on the western edge of Christchurch located within a bend in the Avon River. There is a rose garden, with over 250 varieties, an herb garden, statuary, and a water fountain. However, this is a landscape garden of enormous trees more than anything else, and the overwhelming visual impression one has from a visit is their vertical lines reaching heavenward and their great circumferences. Only the redwood forests of northern California can boast such impressive trees. The visual impression of such size is overpowering. Surrounded on three sides by the Avon River, and with a large variety of colors, the gardens are visually compelling. Like Sydney, a visit to Christchurch's botanic gardens is both impressive and relaxing.

In this chapter, the focus has been on Italian, French, and English pleasure gardens, although the term pleasure garden is obviously only a convenient rather than an entirely descriptive name. While the development of pleasure gardens is associated with great wealth, the aristocracy, the clergy, and the government, the public at large was not overlooked entirely. In order to share the values of pleasure gardens with average citizens, city parks were developed, many along the lines of and influenced by those examined in this chapter. In the following chapter, many of the Western world's most visually compelling city parks will be assessed.

CHAPTER THREE

CITY PARKS

In Chapters Seven and Eight of this book, there will be an examination of the visual persuasiveness of cities both ancient and modern. However, it is obvious already that an essential feature of the visual impact of any city is its green spaces, which are usually city parks. It is the intent of this chapter to provide an assessment of quite an eclectic mix of city parks in many of the world's great cities. As noted in Chapter Two, pleasure gardens were the province of the aristocracy, the church, and the wealthy. Gradually, the needs and concerns of other citizens were acknowledged, and parks were provided in cities for the use of all. Parks provide a visual contrast to the hard surfaces and structures of a city, such as its streets, sidewalks, and buildings. They also offer a glimpse of nature and offer an antidote to the sometimes stifling air of concrete canyons. Perhaps most of all, parks offer a place for the average citizen to get away from the sometimes stressful environs of his or her workplace just to relax. "The pathways, vegetation and fountains of the garden evoke a sense of peacefulness and well-being that leave the visitor with a more benevolent outlook toward one's fellows than one ordinarily has upon entering the park" (Rosenfield 1989, 221). On weekends, especially, parks provide a place of recreation for children and adults as well. Like the pleasure gardens of the previous chapter, city parks feature green lawns, trees and hedges—often in carefully designed parterres—streams, fountains, buildings, and statuary.

European Parks and Gardens

Some pleasure gardens, such as the one at Versailles, began as vast hunting grounds for royalty. While the majority of the city parks to be considered here did not originate in such a way, there is one which did: Berlin's Tiergarten. The name itself—garden of beasts or animals— denotes as much. Berlin has many parks, but the largest and most visually significant is surely the Tiergarten, which stretches out along either side of the Strasse des 17 juni from the Brandenburg Gate in the east to the Zoologischer Garten in the west. In the 17th century, Friedrich I had the park created as a hunting ground. It was fenced in order to keep the

Fig. 3-1 Tiergarten from the Reichstag Dome

animals being hunted from escaping. Friedrich II had little use for hunting and had the Tiergarten landscaped as a pleasure garden for the people of Berlin. It was landscaped again into its present form in the 19th century. Allied bombing in World War II almost leveled the Tiergarten and what was left of the trees was used for firewood in the war's aftermath.

Thanks to a replanting of trees from all over Germany following the war, the Tiergarten has reclaimed its place as one of the central features of the modern city of Berlin. At some 520 acres, it is comparable in size to New York's Central Park and London's Hyde Park. There are no fences any longer, and many small animals still reside in the park, including rabbits and, if scent is any indication, foxes! The Tiergarten resembles an English landscape garden to some extent, with small ponds and open spaces for picnics and sunbathing. However, the vast number of trees in the park are more suggestive of a forest than anything else. Although a main east-west road, Strasse des 17 juni, divides the Tiergarten roughly in half and several other arteries cut through the park converging at the Grosser Stern, one only has to step several yards into the park to feel completely isolated from the city. At the Grosser Stern, a convergence of eight avenues, is located the Siegessäule or Victory Column, which once stood in front of the Reichstag.

The visual impact of the Tiergarten is inescapable. Modern Berlin around the park is a vast collection of buildings and streets, yet one only has to step into the park to experience the tranquility associated with the traditional pleasure garden. The park, along with many other structures rebuilt after World War II, also stands as a testament to the renaissance of this old city. From inside the new glass dome of the Reichstag, the Tiergarten appears as one blanket of green in the center. The Tiergarten, however, is not Berlin's only green space, in spite of being the largest. Perhaps the most notable of the other parks in the city is Volkspark Friedrichshain on the border between the districts of Prenzlauer Berg and Friedrichshain to the east of the city center.

Volkspark Friedrichshain was developed in the mid-19th century to recognize the ascension to the throne of Prussia by Frederick the Great, although its design has been modified since its inception. As will become increasingly evident, city parks in Western Europe were typically done in the English landscape garden style. This style afforded gently rolling hills, broad open spaces and vistas, and water in some form such as ponds, lakes, and fountains. As they did in the Tiergarten, however, the Nazis built flak towers in the park, making it a target for Allied bombing, and the park suffered greatly as a result. In the aftermath of the war, much of the rubble from the bombing was simply piled into mounds, which have been covered now with grass and appear to be natural parts of the landscape. There are ponds and open spaces for sunbathing, as in the Tiergarten, and jogging and bike paths throughout the park. The 130 acre Volkspark is, for all intents and purposes, an English landscape garden. There is a Japanese pavilion and numerous monuments spread about. A special feature of the park that was not destroyed by Allied bombing during the war is the Fairy Tale Fountain with 106 sculptures of characters from traditional German fairy tales. A former swimming pool has been replaced by an outdoor gymnasium (http://www.stadtentwicklung.berlin.de).

In nearby Potsdam, on the southwest border of Berlin, is Sanssouci, the baroque palace of Frederick the Great, complete with terraced formal gardens, a circular pond, and a fountain fronting the palace. Although the palace gardens are beautiful and colorful, the largest park is the New Garden east of the palace, built by Frederick William II at the end of the 18th century. This large park is an English landscape garden, which is now open to the public (http://www.spsg.de). In the spirit of such gardens, there are large open areas, wooded areas, and lakes. The English landscape garden, it will be remembered, was designed to mimic nature and thus the New Garden once included a herd of cows and a dairy.

Fig. 3-2 New Garden Potsdam

Today the park is especially popular with hikers, cyclists, clothed and unclothed sunbathers, and tourists. A regular walking tour of the garden originates in Berlin and takes visitors through the sites, which are especially interesting historically. Unlike other parks modeled after the English landscape garden, the New Garden features several buildings built for the use of Frederick William II and later royals. There were the Marble Palace, the ice house, the Gothic Library, and the Orangery, but most notable was Cecilienhof Palace.

Palace Cecilienhof was built by Emperor Wilhelm II of Germany for his son and his wife Cecilie. It was designed and built in the Tudor style with oak and brick. Historically, Cecilienhof is best known as the location of the Potsdam Conference in the summer of 1945. It was here that American president Harry S. Truman met with British Prime Ministers Winston Churchill and Clement Attlee and Soviet Premier Joseph Stalin to discuss and define the terms for the surrender of Japan at the end of World War II. Beyond the historical significance, these buildings offer another visually persuasive element to the New Garden by their own compelling architecture.

Before leaving Germany, it is important to consider the large public park in Munich known as the English Garden. This 910 acre park

Fig. 3-3 English Garden Munich in Winter

originated in the late 18th century as a military site. From the outset, however, the English Garden was intended for use by the public. Like the New Garden in Potsdam, Munich's English Garden features wide open areas for hiking, cycling, and sunbathing. Also like the New Garden, there are numerous architectural features of the park to capture the visitor's eye: a Japanese tea house, a temple to Apollo called the Monopteros, and a Chinese Tower or pagoda (http://www.muenchen.de).

East of Germany, Prague, in the Czech Republic, is notable for its architecture, but a visitor will also be impressed by the large number of parks in the city. Like Budapest, Hungary, the city of Prague is divided into two main sections by a river, the Vltava (Moldau), with a relatively flat area on one side and a hilly one on the other. The hillside area of the city on the left bank of the river features the vast Prague fortress with its castle and St. Vitus Cathedral. Also on this hillside, to either side of the fortress as well as within it, are three quite visually powerful gardens. To the east of the fortress lies Letná Park, to the southwest lies Petrin Hill, and adjacent to the castle along the wall on the north is the Royal Garden. There are five other gardens associated with the castle, but the Royal Garden is the most significant one in terms of size and design.

Letná Park is a large English landscape garden, although it also contains several plots of flowering plants. From the park, one has a very complete panoramic view of Prague, including especially the Old City. There are several footpaths through the park, and if one were to begin on

Fig. 3-4 Letná Park

the eastern edge and walk west one would easily find the fortress walls and the Royal Garden with its Royal Summer House. Midway through Letná Park, there is a huge working metronome easily visible from below the park and across the river. It stands on the site of a now demolished massive statue of Joseph Stalin.

Arriving at the Royal Garden, one is immediately confronted with flower plots and fountains in the style of the formal French garden, although the entire garden resembles more the English landscape garden. Although this is surely a pleasure garden, the Royal Garden is also a place for study in that there are many deliberate plantings of trees as well as flowers. Further west and south of the fortress and castle is Petrin Hill, which, like Letná Park, is an English landscape garden but also with a large rose garden, a pony ride and concession stand for children, and an observation tower resembling Paris's Eiffel Tower connected to a snack bar with wine and beer available for adults. Petrin Hill may be accessed by a funicular, and several footpaths from the terminus of the funicular to the observation tower lead one past several large plots in the style of the French parterres.

A park similar to the English Garden in Munich may be found in the city of Amsterdam in The Netherlands. Amsterdam is for many people

Fig. 3-5 Royal Garden Prague

already a city of visual splendor. Its many canals, like those in Venice, give the city an aura of stillness and beauty and make it almost unique among the world's great cities. Even Amsterdam, however, needed a park, and so in the mid-19th century a citizen's group formed to purchase land on the western edge of Amsterdam to be developed into a riding and walking area (http://www.amsterdam.info). The group charged a fee for others to use the park. Once the park opened, a statue of the Dutch writer Joost van den Vondel was placed in the park, and subsequently people began to refer to the area as "Vondel's Park" or simply Vondelpark. Vondelpark grew to its present size of 120 acres and, in the 20th century, was donated to the city of Amsterdam. In the park, one may find cycling paths, a rose garden, walking trails, a theatre, and a children's playground.

Farther north, in Stockholm, Sweden, open spaces and green areas complement the already noticeable pleasure garden aspect of the city itself. "One-third of the area within the city limits is made up of water, while while another third comprises parks and woodlands" (Proctor and Roland 2006, 67). Sitting on the water and built on 14 islands, Stockholm offers multiple opportunities to walk over bridges to several of the islands in its harbor, many of which are like parks themselves. On Skeppsholmen, for example, which is home to the Moderna Museet, there is the aura of

Fig. 3-6 King's Gardens Stockholm

visiting a hilly wood. In the city proper, the primary city park is Kungsträdgården or King's Gardens. It is a long rectangle extending from the harbor up a gentle slope to Hamngatan. Today, the park is mostly a paved area providing a place for people to sit, walk, have picnics, and sometimes to listen to itinerant musicians or watch public performances by individuals. Its name notwithstanding, there are no longer any of the King's gardens here, although there are trees along the park's perimeter.

Now moving south to Rome, the Eternal City, there are many green places, some of them quite extensive, but surely the most visually impressive of them all are the Villa Borghese Gardens. In the first part of the 17th century, Cardinal Scipione Borghese, whose uncle was Pope Paul V, began to develop this 148 acre former vineyard as a complement to his Villa Borghese on the Pincio Hill at what was then the northern edge of Rome. Scipione Borghese was a notable art collector and intended the Villa to be a place for entertainment and to house his art collection. Today, the Villa Borghese remains as a museum to display Scipione's collection. Immediately around the Villa are small formal gardens, statuary, and a sizeable greenhouse, but by the 19th century the remainder of the park was redesigned into an English landscape garden. In addition to the usual statuary, trees, and open spaces, there remain in the park wide riding paths

Fig. 3-7 Villa Borghese Gardens

still used by cavalry. The rolling hill location, just north of the Spanish Steps, affords a good vista of the city of Rome (Gilbert and Brouse 2006).

Just as Versailles may be the most magnificent of the great French formal gardens, so Paris may be the most magnificent of European cities from the standpoint of city parks. Paris is for a host of visitors the most beautiful city in the world, a claim to be examined in detail later in this book, and the city's parks are vital aspects of its beauty and visual power. In this part of the chapter, five parks will be examined: the Jardin du Luxembourg, the Parc des Buttes Chaumont, the Jardin des Tuileries, the Jardin des Plantes, and the Bois de Boulogne.

A central reason for the visual persuasiveness of the city of Paris is that, like Berlin, it is an axial city. Cutting through the city from east to west is a central axis from the eastern walls of the Louvre through the Arc de Triomphe to the Grand Arche de la Défense in the west. Much of this axis is formed by the grand avenue known as the Champs Élysées. Walking west away from the Louvre and past the Arche de Triomphe du Carrousel, one emerges into one of the oldest and most beautiful parks in Paris—the Jardin des Tuileries—originally built by Catherine de Medici in the 16th century. It adjoined the Tuileries Palace, which formed the eastern boundary of the Louvre but was later destroyed by fire. Originally an

Fig. 3-8 Jardin des Tuileries

Italian style pleasure garden, it was redesigned during the reign of Louis XIV (http://www.aviewoncities.com).

The park is now a classic French pleasure garden designed by André le Nôtre, the landscape architect of Vaux le Vicomte and Versailles. Bordered on the south by the Quai des Tuileries and the River Seine and on the north by the Rue de Rivoli, the garden ends at the Place de la Concorde which marks the eastern end of the Champs Élysées. On the southern side of the garden at this point is the Orangerie museum and on the northern side is the Jeu de Paume museum. The Jardin des Tuileries itself has a central axis featuring small ponds near each end. From these ponds radiate *allées* to the north and south. The long central axis is wide enough to accommodate walkers as well as joggers. There are formal parterres, trees, and flowers planted all along the route. From the standpoint of visual impact, there are spectacular views of Paris from almost any place in the garden: the Louvre to the east, the Place de la Concorde and its obelisk to the west, the Tour Eiffel to the southwest, and so on.

Across the Seine on the Left Bank and walking uphill, one comes to the large Jardin du Luxembourg. This garden is part of the grounds of the Palais du Luxembourg, built in the 17th century for Marie de Medici. Subsequent modifications to the palace have removed much of its

Fig. 3-9 Jardin du Luxembourg

resemblance to the Pitti Palace in Florence where Marie had grown up, but the garden was suggested by the Pitti's adjacent Boboli Gardens. Today the palace is the home of the French Senate. A large pond with a fountain stands in front and to the center of the palace and is a popular destination for children wishing to sail toy boats. As in the Tuileries garden, wrought iron benches are located around the pond and in the more wooded areas of the park as well. The many trees radiating away from the circular area of the pond make a walk in the park or simple sitting a calming, soothing experience, and the park is a green respite from the hard surfaces of the city's buildings and streets. There are, in the classic French style, parterres de broderie, terraces, and statuary (http://www.aviewoncities.com).

To the east of the Jardin du Luxembourg but still on the Left Bank is the Jardin des Plantes. This garden is the primary French botanical garden and as such is comparable to Kew Gardens in London. Dating to the 17th century, the Jardin des Plantes is part of the French Museum of Natural History, which stands on the western corner of the garden's triangular layout. The southern side of the garden is laid out in successive parterres with dividing crosswalks, while the northern side resembles a series of small interconnected circular planting spaces. There one may find many varieties of flowering plants and hothouses (http://www.paris.fr). The Parc des Buttes Chaumont is located quite a distance north of the previous ones

Fig. 3-10 Parc des Buttes Chaumont

discussed here in the 19th arrondissement. The area is not frequented by tourists as a rule, which is unfortunate considering the visual power of this park. As its name suggests, the park features a notable hill on a partial island in the park's lake. Once the site of gypsum and limestone mining, the Parc des Buttes Chaumont is quite hilly, providing numerous opportunities for climbing or, in the case of children, for sliding down hills. Unlike the other parks and gardens discussed here, this park is more Italian in its style. Its main features are rocks, lawns, and trees. Like other parks, it features monuments and structures, such as a Temple of Sybil on the hill of the island.

Another vast park in Paris is situated on the western edge of the city in the 16th arrondissement. The Bois de Boulogne, as its name suggests, is, like the Tiergarten, a substantial forest with more traditional park features, such as lawns and lakes, carved out of what was once a royal hunting ground (http://www.paris.fr). Although prostitutes ply the park by night, by day it attracts a different clientele. Trails for walking, cycling, rollerblading, and jogging crisscross the Bois, and there are several lakes in addition to the Seine River bordering the park's western edge. The Bois is home to two horse racing venues, Longchamp and Auteuil, and the Roland Garros tennis complex, which hosts the annual internationally known French Open competition. The Bois, like several other city parks, is home to a zoo and children's amusement park on its northern edge.

Fig. 3-11 Bois de Boulogne

Some would argue that it is London, not Paris, which is the most beautiful city in the world. Whatever one's preference may be, London is certainly the equal of Paris when it comes to parks and gardens available to the city's residents. Here, the discussion will center upon the most famous of London's green spaces, Hyde Park, and will include Kensington Gardens, the Green Park, St. James's Park, Regent's Park, and Hampstead Heath. Although they are identified separately today, and for the most part clearly delineated by roads, the first four of these parks originated as one continuous east-west hunting ground for royalty, and that fact makes the four much more alike than different. Henry VIII took the land from the monks of Westminster Abbey and had the area fenced as a hunting enclosure, much like the Tiergarten. Elizabeth I continued the tradition, but by the middle of the 17th century Charles I opened Hyde Park to the public and the fences were eventually removed. Subsequent rulers had the land modified into the English landscape garden style seen today (http://www.royalparks.org.uk).

In addition to gently rolling lawns and many trees, a dramatic feature of Hyde Park is the Serpentine, an S-shaped lake formed by damming a stream which flowed through the park. The park is quite large—350 acres—and is joined on its western edge by Kensington Gardens, which adds another 270 acres to what seems primarily to be one continuous

Fig. 3-12 St. James's Park

designed space. Hyde Park is slightly north and west of the Buckingham Palace grounds, which today separate Hyde Park from the Green Park, north of the palace, and St. James's Park to the east. Numerous walking and jogging paths crisscross all of the parks, and a large lake divides St. James's Park in two sections. The lake itself is in the shape of an open wrench. Many kinds of trees and animals are at home in these parks. Ducks and geese are attracted by the ponds and lakes, and the other fauna include bats, songbirds, squirrels, and the like.

Regent's Park, in the area north of Hyde Park and Marylebone Road, was also a hunting ground of Henry VIII (http://www.royalparks.org.uk). Today, it features a large boating lake and large, open sporting fields for cricket, softball, and football (soccer). There is an open-air theatre, a bandstand, numerous cafés, and not least of all the London Zoo. The 410 acre park also features rose and wildflower gardens. Regent's College is located on the southeastern. All five of these parks taken together give Londoners and visitors to London places of respite from the bustle of the city. They also, like the other city parks examined here, provide a place to socialize, and it is quite common to see multiple groups of people playing games and picnicking together in these areas. In terms of visual persuasion, these parks strongly support the iconicity of the city of London itself.

Finally, London is home to Hampstead Heath on the northern edge of the city. The Heath is much larger than the previously discussed London

Fig. 3-13 Phoenix Park Dublin

parks at 790 acres and is similar to the Bois de Boulogne in Paris in the activities which take place there, although unlike the Bois the Heath is hilly. There are numerous ponds, including separate men's and women's bathing ponds, a model boating pond, and a bird sanctuary pond. There is a bandstand, a concert shell, and several residential structures. Finally, the Heath is still home to deer (muntjac) as well as small mammals such as foxes and hedgehogs (http://www.cityoflondon.gov.uk).

Across the Irish Sea in Dublin, there are two parks worthy of assessment. One is a huge English landscape garden on the northwestern edge of the city called Phoenix Park, and the other is St. Stephen's Green, a much smaller landscape garden in the city center. Phoenix Park is the largest public park in Europe and twice the size of Manhattan's Central Park. Like the London parks taken together and the Tiergarten, it originated as a hunting preserve, in this case for Charles II (http://goireland.about.com). It was protected by stone fencing, seven miles of which may still be seen today, although access to the park is no longer through locked gates. It is a rolling green area with much shrubbery and many trees, and fallow deer still call the park home. While as a public

Fig. 3-14 St. Stephen's Green

park it is the pleasure garden aspect that is most inviting to residents and visitors, there are many different attractions to be found in Phoenix Park: the home of the President of Ireland, a castle, sporting fields for cricket and polo, a B&B, and monuments such as a papal cross, the Wellington Monument, and the Phoenix Monument. Finally, the Dublin Zoo is located here.

Phoenix Park is some distance away from the Dublin city center and is for that reason not readily accessible. Not so St. Stephen's Green, which is within walking distance from most locations in the Dublin center. A much smaller park than Phoenix at 22 acres, St. Stephen's Green could best be described as a rectangular landscape park with flower gardens. It dates to the 17th century and was originally a walled common. On the northern side of the park and stretching across its edge is a large lake, which attracts ducks, geese, and swans. There are recreation and picnicking areas within a surrounding area of trees. At the center of the park is a fountain and formal gardens which provide a profusion of color. Both Phoenix Park and St. Stephen's Green exhibit the green lawns, shrubs, and trees which give Ireland its nickname of the Emerald Isle.

US and Canadian Parks and Gardens

When people visualize Manhattan, several characteristics are inevitable —skyscrapers and the skyline in general, crowds, pavement and concrete—but Manhattan is equally well known for Central Park, in some minds the most famous city park in the world. Central Park was the first large urban landscape park to be built in the United States. Its construction was authorized in 1853 by the New York state legislature. Its now 843 acres was largely unsuitable for commercial or private development due to a terrain of both swamps and bluffs, although it was home to Irish pig farmers and German gardeners who had to be evicted using the principle of eminent domain. Although it appears to be natural, as was the case with the traditional English landscape garden, the park is almost entirely artificial in the sense that it was built according to a juried landscape design (http://www.centralpark.com).

The building of Central Park was a huge undertaking. It required 20,000 or so workers to move almost 3 million cubic yards of soil and to plant over 270,000 trees (http://www.centralpark.com). The park extends from West 59th Street in the south to West 110th Street on the north. Fifth Avenue is the park's eastern border along which one will find The Metropolitan Museum of Art, the Guggenheim Manhattan Museum, and the Frick Museum. Central Park West forms the western border along which one will find the American Museum of Natural History. These iconic museums notwithstanding, it is Central Park itself that is the city's icon. There are attractions within to meet virtually every person's desire. There are numerous bodies of water. Some, like The Pond on the southern end of the park and Turtle Pond further north, are small, while others are huge. Among the larger bodies of water are The Lake, diagonally across Central Park West from the Natural History Museum, and the Jacqueline Kennedy Onassis Reservoir a bit further north and extending across the whole park from west to east.

Numerous paths crisscross Central Park and are regularly used for jogging, cycling, or just walking. There are open lawns for picnickers and for sports such as softball and soccer. Four roads cross the park from east to west. There are many children's playgrounds and the Central Park Zoo. Directly behind the Metropolitan Museum of Art is the Great Lawn, where the New York Philharmonic gives a concert each summer and the Metropolitan Opera stages two operas. Of course, the park has hosted numerous outdoor popular music concerts by such artists as Barbara Streisand, Elton John, Simon and Garfunkel, and Bon Jovi among others. The Delacorte Theater in the park is home to the New York Shakespeare

Festival. Numerous statues grace the park as is typical of great city parks, and one will find a large variety of birds, raccoons, squirrels, chipmunks, and opossums.

Much smaller than Central Park, but nonetheless distinctive, Battery Park could be called Manhattan's front door inasmuch as it sits at the tip of the island and faces New York harbor. Covering 25 acres, Battery Park is reminiscent of the early Italian pleasure gardens. Its lawns and trees offer a comparatively quiet and serene respite from the stresses of the city. Numerous memorials adorn the park. The Battery was originally the location of cannon emplacements for the protection of the city from naval invasion, hence its name.

Down the east coast from Manhattan is the US Capitol in Washington, DC. Perhaps the best known public space in the District is the National Mall, a long rectangular park stretching from the Capitol to the Washington Monument. While this area is popularly called the Mall, in truth the National Mall extends on to the Lincoln Memorial as well as from the White House to the Jefferson Memorial. It certainly is a park in the sense that it attracts joggers, cyclists, and pedestrians, but it is more an open space than a traditional landscape park in spite of trees planted along the Mall's perimeter. More than other parks, however, the National Mall is a "monument center" (http://www.nationalmall.org) and grows more crowded with memorials with each passing decade. Along its perimeter also are the various museums of the Smithsonian complex. The Mall is distinctive among the city parks being examined here in that it has served so often for huge gatherings of citizens who come to the District for large rallies, often of a decidedly political nature. The area of the Mall surrounding the Tidal Basin and including the Jefferson Memorial and the Franklin D. Roosevelt Memorial is quite unique and popular among tourists in the Spring in that it is planted with flowering Japanese cherry trees.

Perhaps the most traditional city park in the District is Rock Creek Park extending some 12 miles from the Potomac River to the District's border with Maryland (http://dc.about.com). A huge traditional English landscape garden, Rock Creek Park provides space for walking, jogging, hiking, biking, horseback riding, and the like. Much of the park is densely wooded, like the Bois de Boulogne in Paris. There are over 25 miles of trails within the park, as well as a nature center, flower gardens, amphitheater, tennis center, and golf course. Rock Creek Park is also the home of the National Zoo. The remainder of the US is also scattered with cities both large and small that are home to parks and gardens of note.

Fig. 3-15 Leu Gardens Orlando

Among these are Chicago, Orlando, San Antonio, Los Angeles, and San Francisco.

Chicago, Illinois, is akin to Manhattan in the presence of one skyscraper after another, yet it is also home to numerous parks and gardens for its residents and visitors. Most notable of these parks is Grant Park adjacent to the shores of Lake Michigan in the center of the city's so-called Loop. Grant Park is a vast 319 acre open green space interspersed with monuments and memorials and home to the Art Institute, Adler Planetarium, the Field Museum of Natural History, and the Shedd Aquarium. An essentially flat entity, Grant Park, like the National Mall, has been a venue for political demonstrations, concerts, and festivals. There are numerous trees and shrubs in the park and a number of colorful flower gardens, but the visual impression of the park is of a broad and long green vista. Buckingham Fountain in the park is one of the largest in the world. Numerous monuments adorn Grant Park, including an Abraham Lincoln monument and a Christopher Columbus monument.

Orlando, Florida, home to Disney World as well as Universal Studios and other amusement parks, is like Stockholm in that the city itself, were it not so populated with hotels and skyscrapers, is a park. Whereas Stockholm sits on 14 islands, much of Orlando is built on reclaimed land

Fig. 3-16 Bellingrath Gardens

that once was swampy and largely uninhabitable. It is the climate and abundance of water that makes Orlando an excellent place to find parks and especially gardens. One such place, once private but now the property of the city, is Leu Gardens. The location is also the former home of Harry P. and Mary Jane Leu. Mr. Leu, a wealthy industrial supply merchant, bought the property in 1936, although the grounds and home date to the late 19th century. The Leus donated the property to the City of Orlando in 1961. Leu is quite different from the other city parks discussed here. It is more akin to the traditional English flower garden than anything else, although it is 30 acres in size. In actuality, the property is a large number of small gardens connected by crisscrossing paths. It borders Lake Rowena. These gardens reflect the Leus' personal interests and insure that at any time of the year one will find flowering plants abloom. A partial list of these gardens tells the tale: a citrus grove—especially appropriate for Orlando, which was formerly heavily identified with orange groves—an herb garden, a vegetable garden, a butterfly garden, a rose garden, a floral clock, and the largest camellia garden in the Eastern US. Except for the heat and humidity which are endemic to Orlando in the summer and offset somewhat by the trees of the location, a stroll through the Leu Gardens is a lesson in the visual persuasiveness of designed spaces (http://www. leugardens.org).

Like Florida, Alabama is a Gulf Coast state, and Theodore, which is south of Mobile on the coast, is home to one of the most popular tourist attractions in the south: Bellingrath Gardens. The 65 acre park, which includes the mansion built by the Bellingraths in 1935, is vast and heavily wooded, suggesting an English landscape garden design. However, the park, like Leu Gardens, is primarily a number of flower gardens connected together with crisscrossing pathways. It is the flowers that bring the visitors any time of the year: camellias, azaleas, roses, tulips, Easter lilies, chrysanthemums, and the like. There is also an Oriental garden, Mirror Lake, and Mermaid Pool (http://www.bellingrath.org).

By contrast to the semi-tropical locale of central Florida and the waterside locale of southern Alabama, the city of San Antonio, Texas, is almost arid and much of the year is quite hot. Perhaps as a result of its climate as much as its geography, San Antonio has developed parks and gardens that do an excellent job of providing shade. Perhaps the most familiar such "park," although some would not think of it as one, is the Paseo del Rio or Riverwalk. To be sure, the Riverwalk is heavily commercialized, being lined with restaurants, hotels, and other commercial establishments on both sides of the San Antonio river. However, it is not just these businesses that bring visitors to the Riverwalk, it is as much the cool waterside walkways and shade trees.

The San Antonio River flows through the city's downtown area and brought serious flooding until the early part of the 20th century when plans began to be made to control the flow of the river through a set of dams and diversion channels. The result is the Riverwalk, which is one story below street level in the city's center. The width and depth of the river are strictly controlled and silt is removed annually to keep the attraction comparatively clean. Paved and bricked pathways line either side of the Riverwalk, and twenty bridges facilitate movement across the stream. For entertainment, small passenger boats, some with bands aboard, ply the river (http://www.thesanantonioriverwalk.com). The visitor can use this park for relaxation, recreation, entertainment, and fine dining. The Riverwalk is an especially attractive venue during the Christmas season, when its trees, bridges, and commercial establishments are lavishly decorated with lights and bunting.

A map of Los Angeles, California, with parks and gardens highlighted, looks like a polka dot fabric. Perhaps the best known of the parks and gardens is the more than 4,000 acre Griffith Park and urban wilderness area, while one of the smallest but most attractive ones is Exposition Park adjacent to the University of Southern California in downtown Los Angeles. Then, to the northeast of the city itself in the suburb of San Marino, near Pasadena, are the Botanical Gardens of the Huntington Library. Griffith Park is part of the foothills of the Santa Monica mountains, thus it is quite hilly in addition to being heavily wooded in places. Pathways through the hills provide ample opportunities for hikers, joggers, and cyclists. As might be expected in such a large park,

Fig. 3-17 Huntington Gardens

there are multiple entertainment venues, such as the Los Angeles Zoo, a merry-go-round and pony rides, a miniature train ride, golf courses, a Greek Theatre, the Gene Autry Museum of the American West, and the renowned Griffith Observatory. Like many other locations in the Los Angeles area, Griffith Park has been the location of a number of film shoots (http://www.discoverlosangeles.com).

Exposition Park is a 160 acre site that is home to a large number of cultural facilities. These facilities include Los Angeles Memorial Coliseum, the Natural History Museum of Los Angeles County, the California Science Center, the California African-American Museum, a farmers market, and, most importantly for the purposes of this chapter, a seven acre sunken rose garden built in an area which was formerly a horse racing track. The rose garden has more than 20,000 bushes and some 200 varieties of roses. It also has a gazebo, a central fountain, and a number of statues, which make the garden a popular location for wedding photography and picnics (http://www.discoverlosangeles.com).

In San Marino, adjacent to Pasadena, California, Henry Huntington, a wealthy railroad executive, art, and book collector, built an estate which is now an art museum, a library of rare books, and nearly 600 acres of botanical gardens (http://www.huntington.org). About 120 acres of the botanical gardens have been landscaped and planted and are open to the public. Like Leu Gardens and Bellingrath Gardens, this park is a set of flower gardens of various types. Some of these are a camellia garden, Chinese garden, Jungle Garden, lily ponds, a rose garden, and an herb garden. The Huntington botanical gardens are colorful at any time of the year and are a popular destination for the many bus tours which ply the southern California highways. The estate itself has been a popular location for film and television shoots. Because of the location's similarity in appearance to south Florida, the television series *CSI: Miami* has sometimes used the gardens for an episode.

A map of San Francisco, California, with its parks highlighted is also like a polka dot fabric. In terms of location, the most dramatic of these parks is the Presidio, formerly a military post, which lies directly on San Francisco Bay and from which one accesses the Golden Gate Bridge. Several blocks south of the Presidio is San Francisco's premier park: Golden Gate Park. This 1,017 acre rectangular park is reminiscent in appearance of Manhattan's Central park and was built with many of the same fundamental ideas in mind. Begun in the mid-18th century by John McLaren, Golden Gate Park was originally a wasteland of scrub oaks and sand dunes. Today, the English landscape style park is also home to several museums and similar attractions. Among these are the California Academy of Sciences, the De Young Museum, the Children's Playground and Carrousel, the Music Concourse, the National AIDS Memorial Grove, a Japanese Tea Garden, and a Bison Paddock still in use. The park also attracts the usual denizens of city parks: cyclists, joggers, walkers, and picnickers (http://www.sfrecpark.org).

Alamo Square is much smaller than Golden Gate Park but is almost equally attractive to visitors for two reasons. Its hilltop location provides a panoramic view of the city, and the surrounding residential area is especially scenic because of the many colorful and architecturally impressive Victorian homes along the streets. These include a group of Queen Anne style homes known as the Painted Ladies, which have appeared in television series and films as well as postcards of the city. The park encompasses four city blocks and is mostly open lawn and trees. However, there are also children's playgrounds, a play area for dogs, tennis courts, picnic tables, and flower beds. Alamo Square was an important refuge area for citizens displaced by the 1906 earthquake which destroyed much of the city (http://www.sfrecpark.org).

Before leaving North America to talk about city parks in Australia and New Zealand, a visit to the Canadian province of Québec is in order to assess parks in Montreal and Québec City. Montreal's name is, of course,

Fig. 3-18 Mount Royal Park Montreal

French and refers to the mountain above the city's center. Although actually only a hill, "mont réal" is also a large city park. The park begins at a lower level of the hill and extends upward to the summit. It is cut through with trails, stairs, and bridges for walkers, and a dirt road winds up through the heavily wooded park. At the summit is Beaver Lake, where in the winter Montrealers may ice skate. Also in the winter months, snow in the park affords an opportunity for cross-country skiing. Mount Royal Park was designed by Frederick Law Olmsted, who had designed Manhattan's Central Park. As it is the highest point in the city, the park affords a number of spectacular overviews of Montreal.

Spectacular views from a hilltop location are perhaps the defining feature of the walled fortress of Québec City, the only such walled city in North America. There are two distinct areas of Québec City: a lower city and an upper one. On the uppermost part of the upper city is a walled fortress or citadel but also the visually impressive Hôtel du Parlement, the grounds of which are a beautiful example of an English flower garden. In the street fronting the national assembly building is the huge Fontaine de Tourny. Below this garden on the way back to the lower city, one comes to the famous hotel Chateau Frontenac. The upper city from the park affords scenic views of the St. Lawrence River below and the residences across the river.

City Parks of Australia and New Zealand

Fig. 3-19 Hyde Park Sydney

Although thousands of miles away from any of the city parks and gardens which have been examined to this point, Sydney and Melbourne, Australia, and Wellington, New Zealand, provide comparable examples of city parks worth examination. Sydney's royal botanic gardens, treated in the preceding chapter, abut an almost equally vast city park called The Domain. This area was originally for the exclusive use of the governor, whose residence until 1996 was located in the park. It is characterized by open lawns sparsely populated by palms and other trees, and it provides areas for cricket, strolling, jogging, picnicking, and sunbathing. The Domain is also home to the Art Gallery of New South Wales on its eastern edge.

As one continues to walk past the art gallery and St. Mary's Cathedral and onward toward the center of the city of Sydney, one comes to another significant city park. This one is Hyde Park, named after its London counterpart. Hyde Park, like The Domain, is primarily lawn with a fringe of trees. However, it has at its center the large and visually impressive bronze and granite Archibald Fountain, which commemorates the World

War I alliance of Australia and France. Closer to the city center is the Anzac Memorial dedicated to Australian servicemen who died for their country. Both The Domain and Hyde Park are close enough to Sydney's commercial center that businesspeople can and do flock to these gardens for their shelter in the summer and for lunch breaks.

South and west along the coast from Sydney is Australia's "other" large city: Melbourne. Perhaps Melbourne's most impressive landscape garden is the King's Domain mentioned in the previous chapter. This park lying between the Yarra River and St. Kilda Road is just south of the Melbourne city center. There are roads and paths through the park, with many places for picnicking, walking, and jogging. Like The Domain in Sydney, the King's Domain is the location on a hilltop of Government House, the residence of the governor of Victoria. Another large structure in the park is the Shrine of Remembrance, honoring Australian soldiers who died in battle. Finally, there is the Sidney Myer Music Bowl.

Carlton Gardens, north of Victoria Street and the Melbourne city center, is a smaller but almost equally impressive rectangular park laid out in the English landscape garden style. Dating to the end of the 19th century, the park is also the location of the Royal Exhibition Building and the Melbourne Museum. It is a city park that attracts sunbathers, joggers, or just those out for a stroll.

Pleasure gardens, the subject of the previous chapter, originated as places for royalty and clergy to relax, entertain, and contemplate matters both private and public. With the passage of time, and with the waning of both royal and ecclesiastical power, parks and gardens were provided for the use of all citizens and for the same purposes. Some of these city parks were originally for the royalty, such as the parks of London, and were simply given to the public, while others, like Manhattan's Central Park, were deliberately built for the edification of the public. The majority of the city parks assessed in this chapter have been built in the style of the English landscape garden, which seems to afford the broadest set of recreational uses of parks. Visually, all parks are impressive spaces. They offer color ranging from the green of lawns and trees to the variety of colors of specialized flower planting. They provide the coolness of ponds and the visual delight of fountains. They provide the visitor with the respite needed from the harsh angularity of a city's structures and the stress of its commercial transactions.

CHAPTER FOUR

NATIONAL PARKS

The National Parks of the United States, and the related National Monuments, could readily be seen as or treated here as simple extensions of the idea of city parks and gardens. In other words, they could be seen as places offering respite, relaxation, recreation, and entertainment, which of course they do among other things. However, the idea of the national park in the US did not originate in the same way as did the idea of the city park. Only later did the national parks provide for recreation and entertainment, almost as an afterthought. The original idea, called America's best idea by Wallace Stegner (Duncan and Burns 2009), was a unique one intellectually, historically, and culturally and quite different from the ideas which motivated the designed spaces treated heretofore in this book. Indeed, the national parks and monuments of the US are actually not designed spaces at all but discovered spaces, although to be sure the development of a national park does require the addition of carefully designed roads, trails, and buildings.

The expansion of America from east to west revealed many areas of the country that were not only visually spectacular but also unique in the world. Certainly, there were no comparable places to be found in Europe. Because of their spectacle and uniqueness, early explorers and travelers felt the need to preserve these areas and protect them from development so that others could encounter and enjoy them. Many Americans felt that the country had failed to preserve and protect the most visually spectacular site in the East, Niagara Falls, and wished to avoid repeating that error. At Niagara Falls, businesses and industries had been allowed to build near the site and within the view of visitors to the falls (Runte 2010). And so it was that first the state of California and almost immediately thereafter the US Congress enacted laws to set aside Western sites for preservation and protection, and the National Park Service was established in 1916. However, there is more to the establishment of national parks than merely guaranteeing that certain sites be preserved for the enjoyment of all. The national parks came not only to be America's best idea but a singular cultural icon.

As a young nation, America in the last quarter of the 18th century had no cultural icons compared to Europe. Indeed, when France was asked by the Colonies to support the American Revolution, she requested some

Fig. 4-1 Yellowstone Geyser Basin

justification for the risk she would be taking (Runte 2010). This request came during a period when the budding nation also was being routinely taken to task by such European writers as Count de Buffon and Abbé Raynal for its lack of cultural icons that could compare to those of Europe. No less a figure than Thomas Jefferson attempted a justification for France and indirectly for America's outright critics in his *Notes on the State of Virginia* in 1780. Jefferson could not offer any examples of an American mathematician, or poet, or painter, or architect comparable to those of Europe, although he did mention George Washington in the conduct of war and Benjamin Franklin in physics. Instead, Jefferson sought refuge in what America had. Although the great lands of the West that would become the first national parks had yet to be discovered, Jefferson offered up the Potomac River and the Shenandoah Valley, making the argument for perhaps the first time that it was scenery that was the source of America's cultural status. It was an argument that proved not to be refutable within a hundred years.

Although the history of national park development is fascinating, it is not the focus of this chapter. For those interested in this history, Alfred Runte's *National Parks* (2010) is indispensable. Then there is Dayton Duncan and Ken Burns's illustrated history *The National Parks: America's Best Idea* (2009), which is based on Burns's twelve-hour PBS film series written by Duncan and co-produced by the two men. This

Fig. 4-2 Yellowstone Mammoth Hot Springs

book's illustrations are a wonderful extension of the images in this chapter. There are now so many national parks that it is also not possible in the space available here to consider them all as examples of visual persuasion. There are almost 400 national parks encompassing 84 million acres (Duncan and Burns 2009). With the selected ones included here, therefore, the task will be to examine the visual components which led the parks to be thought of as spectacular and worthy of being set aside for all to enjoy. This is no mean task, for the typical first reaction to a national park is a kind of awe and wonder that make it difficult to find words to express one's thoughts and feelings. The first park to be considered is also the first to be designated a national park in 1872. It is Yellowstone, located in northwestern Wyoming but spilling over into Montana and Idaho. It covers over 2, 200,000 acres (Newhouse 1997).

One can find in Yellowstone all of the features in the man-made city parks of the preceding chapter. There are great open lawns, thick wooded areas, and abundant water. More than in man-made parks, there are large varieties of both flora and fauna, the latter including gray wolves, grizzly bears, brown bears, mule deer, eagles, trumpeter swan, osprey, elk, and bison. Unlike man-made parks, however, Yellowstone is located on the Yellowstone Plateau, which averages about 8,000 feet in elevation above sea level, and it is surrounded by the mountains of the central Rockies. Although it is not so easily accessible as a city park, Yellowstone offers

Fig. 4-3 Yellowstone Falls

similar opportunities for relaxation and recreation and for viewing the beauty of nature. However, these are only the secondary reasons for traveling to visit Yellowstone. Additionally, the park offers several singular and stunning visual features.

The most famous of these visual features is surely Old Faithful Geyser. The park sits on an active geothermal area known as a caldera formed by a supervolcano that has erupted several times in the geological past. The geothermal area is characterized by geysers which periodically spray hot, pressurized water into the air from the depths of heated pools below. Although Yellowstone has many geysers, the best known is Old Faithful, which erupts at about 90 minute intervals. Visitors wait patiently to photograph its plume of water, a sight that has been featured on posters advertising the park for many years. The vertical line of the plume certainly contributes to its visual power. The uniqueness of geysers in general also contributes to the visual effect.

Other geothermal features of the park include a variety of mud pots and also Mammoth Hot Springs. Throughout the park, there are areas where visitors may see mud pots, which are places where sulfurous steam regularly bubbles up through clay from underground. While the mud pots, which resemble a bubbling stew on a stove written large, are fascinating to watch, small children have been observed to become nauseated by the rotten-egg smell of the sulfur! Mammoth Hot Springs is terraced multicolored travertine with steaming pools and small waterfalls. Its visual power derives in part from its immensity and its horizontal spread.

Getting away from the active geothermal features, there is at Specimen Ridge in the northeastern part of the park a large variety of petrified plant species, including redwoods as well as over 100 other plants (Newhouse 1997). This area is warmer and drier than the center of the park and is an area for retreat in the winter for many of the park's large animals. It has large areas of grassland for grazing. Finally, there are the interconnected Yellowstone River, Lake, and falls of the Grand Canyon of the Yellowstone.

Yellowstone Lake is the largest lake in the US at an elevation above 7,000 feet (Newhouse 1997). The Grand Canyon is located north of the lake and features two sets of falls, the upper and the lower, the latter of which at 308 feet is more than double the height of Niagara Falls. While the canyon formed at this part of the river resembles geologically that of the Grand Canyon of the Colorado, another national park, it is only fractionally as large and much narrower. Of course, travelers flock to Yellowstone for many reasons, but it is perhaps the combination of visually spectacular open areas, forests, mountains, geysers, and mud pots as well as an abundance of flora and fauna not easily seen in many other areas of the US that make Yellowstone the visually persuasive site that it is.

Only ten miles south of Yellowstone, and therefore an easily accessible park for travelers either heading to or leaving Yellowstone, is Grand Teton National Park. The Teton Range is a 40 mile long section of the Rocky Mountains. The park is named after the tallest mountain in this range, Grand Teton, which is 13, 770 feet high (Newhouse 1997). It is flanked on the north by Mount Owen and on the south by Middle Teton and South Teton. The latter two, along with Grand Teton, were allegedly referred to by French Canadian trappers as *les trois tétons* or, in English, the three breasts (http://www.ohranger.com). This national park is essentially only a mountain range, but within this range are many of the flora and fauna of Yellowstone, as well as lakes and glaciers. There are moose, coyote, pronghorn antelope, sandhill cranes, and Canada geese. What is so visually dramatic about Grand Teton National Park, however, is how it rises suddenly from the flat valley of Jackson Hole. It has no foothills, so that the uprising is immediate and stark. "The Tetons are fault-block mountains. About five to nine million years ago, two blocks of the earth's crust began to shift along a fault line, one tilting down while the other went up" (Newhouse 1997, 280). In the Jackson Hole valley below, there is the Snake River curling through sagebrush and aspen trees.

Fig. 4-4 Yosemite El Capitan

Grand Teton National Park offers spectacular views of mountains, lakes, and glaciers for visitors driving through the park, although the roads are confined to the valley. A drive through the park provides many different perspectives on the mountains themselves and leads to trailheads for hikers and climbers. The road leads to Jenny Lake, a popular place to swim in warmer weather. Across the lake is Inspiration Point, from which one can see the lake, and the nearby Hidden Falls. Continuing north on the road brings the visitor to Jackson Lake, the largest body of water in the park, which has been enlarged by a dam built before the area was designated as a national park (Newhouse 1997). For the visitor seeking recreation, Grand Teton National Park offers many hiking trails and rock climbing opportunities. Canoeing and fishing are also available as well as camping and backpacking.

Although Yellowstone was the first to be designated a national park, Yosemite is perhaps the prototypical national park. It was identified and set aside by the state of California as a state park before Yellowstone was made the first national park, and it was quickly added to the list of national parks shortly after Yellowstone. It shares many of its features with Yellowstone and is also popular as a rock climbing venue. The park covers over 748,000 acres of largely mountainous wilderness in the Sierra Nevada range of east central California (Newhouse 1997). Yosemite is filled with granite peaks, waterfalls, giant Sequoia trees, and an abundance of wildlife. Its approximately 800 miles of hiking trails give visitors a chance to see mule deer, black bears, marmots, bobcats, cougars, gray foxes, and a large variety of birds along with many other species of animals and flora.

The most popular destination in Yosemite is Yosemite Valley, a mile wide, seven mile long canyon overseen by various peaks including Half Dome and El Capitan. El Capitan's 7,569 foot granite peak has a 3,593 foot vertical wall that is a favorite destination for mountain climbers. Just north of the valley is the highest waterfall in North America. At 2,425 feet, Yosemite Falls has upper, middle, and lower falls, which are also popular tourist destinations (Newhouse 1997). Beyond the valley, there are numerous other falls and a variety of mountain overlooks. Additionally, there are three groves of giant Sequoia trees. The Mariposa Grove of some 200 trees includes the Grizzly Giant, which is over 2,700 years old. The Wawona Tunnel Tree, although fallen in 1969, is also here. This tree became a famous photographic subject when a tunnel for buggies and cars was cut into its base, although the tunnel was harmful to the tree itself.

Yosemite is open throughout the year and offers many opportunities for entertainment to visitors. There is mountain and rock climbing, hiking, and backpacking as previously noted, as well as bus tours, ice fishing, horseback riding, swimming, and cross-country skiing. Merely seeing the many areas of the park would require several days of riding and walking. Like Yellowstone and so many of the national parks, Yosemite is a visual spectacle. Its vertical and horizontal vistas are vast and replete with forest greenery and mountain wildflowers. Its waterfalls and pools offer the calm refreshment that refugees from cities long for. California is home also to several other national parks, including Sequoia and Kings Canyon, Redwood, Death Valley, and Joshua Tree. The first three of these are, like Yosemite, primarily wilderness areas, while the last two are desert parks.

Redwood National Park lies at the extreme northwest edge of California near its border with Oregon. This park features the remnants of what was once a two million acre forest which was nearly decimated by logging (Newhouse 1997). Redwood trees are the tallest trees in the world, some of which attain a height of 378 feet (http://www.visitsequoia.com). Giant redwoods, as they are most often called (*sequoia sempervirens*), are sometimes confused with giant sequoias (*sequoiadendron giganteum*), but they are not the same. Giant sequoias require different climatic conditions than giant redwoods, thus they flourish in different areas of California. Redwoods thrive in a moist, coastal climate, while sequoias live at a higher elevation on the western side of the Sierra Nevada mountain range. While redwoods grow taller, sequoias are larger. Redwoods have a base reaching 22 feet in diameter, while sequoias may reach 40 feet. Both are long lived. Redwoods may reach 2000 years of age and sequoias 3000 years. Obviously, visitors come to Redwood National Park to see these huge redwood trees and to experience their height and massive size. The park also permits backpacking, overnight camping, hiking, horseback riding, and fishing.

South of Yosemite National Park is Sequoia National Park, which is dedicated to preserving the remaining sequoias as Redwood preserves the remaining redwoods. The visual experience of these trees is also awe-inspiring. Most of this park is wilderness, and backpacking is allowed. Sequoia National Park is home to the General Sherman Tree, which is "the world's largest tree and the largest living thing on earth" (Newhouse 1997, 253). It lies in the area of the park known as the Giant Forest. This tree is perhaps 2700 years old and stands over 274 feet tall. Surely there are few things in nature with such commanding visual power. Abutting the park on its northern side is Kings Canyon National Park. The two parks are administered together and for all intents and purposes are a single park. Although Kings Canyon National Park is also home to groves of sequoias, it features the U-shaped canyon of the south fork of the Kings River with sheer rock walls reminiscent of those to be found in Yosemite. Fishing, horseback riding, and cross-country skiing are available to visitors in addition to hiking and backpacking. These wilderness areas in northern and central California give way in the southern part of the state to the strikingly different terrain and visual experiences of deserts.

Death Valley is one of the most singular of all the national parks in its geology and topography being essentially a sandy desert. In the lower 48 states, it is the largest national park comprising approximately 3.3 million acres (Newhouse 1997). Not only is Death Valley the driest and hottest spot in North America, at 282 feet below sea level it is the lowest point in the Western Hemisphere. In spite of its name, Death Valley has a surprising amount of both flora and fauna. There are more than 900 types of plants and a healthy collection of reptiles, kit foxes, coyotes, and bobcats. On the peaks of the surrounding mountains, there are desert bighorn sheep. Because of its harsh climate, Death Valley does not afford visitors many opportunities for recreation, although camping and hiking are popular. What it does offer are vistas of wildflowers in the spring, beds of rock salt crystals, such as the Devil's Golf Course, varicolored sedimentary rock, the remains of borax mines, and refreshingly the springs at Furnace Creek oasis.

The most southerly of California's national parks, Joshua Tree, also consists of desert land. The Mojave Desert and the Colorado Desert come together within the park and provide the visitor with distinctly different experiences. The Colorado in the east is the western part of the Sonoran Desert and is more arid and hotter than the Mojave. The Mojave is higher in elevation and wetter than the Colorado and has more vegetation (Newhouse 1997). However, the area is known and named for the huge yuccas known as Joshua Trees which permeate the western sections of the park. These plants may reach a height of 50 feet and live for more than 200 years. Like Death Valley, this park is primarily accessible by automobile, although some visitors choose mountain bikes to explore its many visual attractions. Large granite formations in the park attract many rock climbers each year.

Fig. 4-5 Grand Canyon

East of these California desert national parks lies the Colorado Plateau, a high desert drained by the Colorado River (Newhouse 1997). It "teems with scenic treasures. Numerous gorges slice the colorfully layered rock; stairstep terraces, buttes, and spires embellish it. The region contains the nation's largest concentration of national parks" (139). The most famous of the Colorado Plateau national parks is Grand Canyon, which Teddy Roosevelt called "the one great sight . . . every American should see." In this section of the chapter, the Grand Canyon will be the first of the national parks to be considered followed by Zion, Bryce Canyon, and the Petrified Forest National Parks, although there are many other such parks and national monuments within an easy drive from these.

Fig. 4-6 More Grand Canyon

This book is about the visual persuasiveness of designed spaces, and throughout there has been an effort made to capture the idea of compelling visual forms and to describe how and why these forms are persuasive. Nowhere else in the book, however, is this idea so evident than in the case of the Grand Canyon. It is at once the quintessential example of what it means for designed space to be visually compelling, which may entirely explain Teddy Roosevelt's admonition. There is, indeed, nothing like it anywhere else in the world. The Grand Canyon is enormous, so that it is impossible for one to take it all in at a single glance no matter where one stands. The canyon is 277 river miles long, 18 miles wide, and one mile deep (http://www.nps.gov/grca). It is because of this great enormity and the fact that it cannot all be comprehended at once that one's first view of the Grand Canyon is likely to be quite literally breathtaking. Following this experience—clearly persuasive as the term is used here—virtually all sights will probably be measured against this yardstick.

The Grand Canyon is so large that it offers a multitude of different vistas. The most popular visit is to the South Rim of the canyon, where one may take both the West Rim and the East Rim Drives for a variety of views. The South Rim is open all year. Quite a different perspective on the canyon, although equally dramatic, may be seen from the North Rim, although this side of the canyon is closed during the winter due to heavy snow. There are a variety of activities available for those who wish to do more than merely view the Grand Canyon. Mule rides and hiking trails lead to the Colorado River at the bottom, and there are also hiking trails to the bottom. Rafting the river is popular with some visitors.

Due north of the Grand Canyon in the state of Utah lie Zion and Bryce Canyon National Parks, both of which are parks featuring visually striking canyons. Zion was originally named "Little Zion" by the Mormons who saw it as akin to the scriptural heavenly city. While the Grand Canyon is most often viewed from above looking down, Zion is most frequently seen from the floor of the canyon, where there are "thick stands of Fremont cottonwood, box elder, willow, and, a short distance away, cactus and thorny mesquite trees. Vegetation changes rapidly as the terrain rises almost a mile in elevation. The high plateaus support Douglas-fir and ponderosa pine" (Newhouse 1997, 204). The canyon was carved by the flow of the Virgin River and features sheer cliffs, some of which exceed 3000 feet. As at other similar parks, hiking, horseback riding, cycling, and cross-country skiing are popular activities.

Fig. 4-7 Bryce Canyon Hoodoos

Bryce Canyon is quite different from Zion and a visual spectacle all its own. Like the Grand Canyon, Bryce was formed largely by erosion, but what erosion formed in Bryce Canyon is a unique "wilderness of phantom-like rock spires, or hoodoos . . . fluted walls and sculptured pinnacles" (Newhouse 1997, 146). Viewed from above at Bryce Point, the Amphitheater looks like the floor of a cave with stalagmites covering the ground. Although there are some of the usual park activities available, Bryce Canyon is almost purely a visual experience with awe-inspiring views. The Amphitheater encompasses six square miles, and especially at sunrise the yellow and amber colors of the park are most pleasing.

East and somewhat north of Bryce Canyon are two more Utah national parks worthy of consideration for their striking visual contents. The first of these is Arches National Park. In this national park is the world's largest collection of natural arches—more than 2000 in all. Like other natural phenomena in the national parks of the Colorado Plateau, Arches is the product of erosion, but in this case the erosion was probably primarily the result of wind eating away at vertical slabs of red sandstone such that arches were left. Perhaps the most commonly seen images of Arches are of Delicate Arch, Landscape Arch, and Double O Arch, but there are other visually dramatic artifacts as well such as Balanced Rock and Mule's Ear Tower (http://www.nps.gov).

Nearby is the much larger Canyonlands National Park. Like the Grand Canyon, Canyonlands is the result of the erosive power of the Colorado River and to a lesser extent the Green River. In many ways, then, this national park features visual images reminiscent of the other parks of the Colorado Plateau. Monument Basin, from Grand View Point for example, is similar to the Grand Canyon. The area known as The Needles features sandstone spires similar to those in Bryce Canyon, as well as Mesa Arch and Angel Arch (http://www.nps.gov).

Southeast of the Grand Canyon is Petrified Forest National Park and its Painted Desert wilderness. The visual attraction of this park is the huge collection of petrified wood, the largest in the world. "Ninety-nine percent of the park's petrified wood comes from tall conifers called *Araucarioxylon*, which resembled modern Norfolk Island pines. These ancient trees grew 200 million years ago in distant highlands, where floods or perhaps mudflows uprooted them" (Newhouse 1997, 197). The petrified trees are principally to be found in the southern areas of the park, while the northern section is a wilderness area known as the Painted Desert. Here the visitor may see the varicolored strata of hills that appear to have been produced by paint and a brush.

Three national parks lie in the Chihuahuan Desert of the Southwest. The northernmost of these, lying in the southeast corner of New Mexico, is Carlsbad Caverns. Just across the Texas border from New Mexico is Guadalupe Mountains National Park, and at the border of Texas with Mexico, where the Rio Grande River makes a sharp turn to the left on its trip to the Gulf of Mexico, is Big Bend. "Water sculptured these

Fig. 4-8 Carlsbad Caverns Hall of Giants

landscapes. A reef from an ancient sea forms the 50-mile-long Guadalupe mountain chain. The seeping of water over millions of years created the cool, dark world of Carlsbad Caverns. Rivers etched out the dramatic canyons of Big Bend" (Newhouse 1997, 111).

Will Rogers is said to have called Carlsbad Caverns the Grand Canyon with a roof (Newhouse 1997). This view has some merit in that the caverns are so vast. There are over 118 known caves that are Carlsbad Caverns, and the caves are certainly colorful. On the other hand, the stalagmites and stalactites that are the predominant visual attractions resemble more the hoodoos of Bryce Canyon than they do anything in the Grand Canyon. Water dripping through limestone "picks up calcite crystals. . . . then releases the crystals with each drop, splattering them onto the floor as the water drips—producing a stalagmite—or leaving them on the ceiling . . . creating a stalactite" (Newhouse 1997, 124). Although an elevator is available to take visitors directly to the Big Room, Carlsbad's largest interior space, the more dramatic visual experience is to be had by walking down the main corridor from the Natural Entrance at the Bat Cave. The park is home in the summer to some half million Mexican free-tailed bats, and the flight of these mammals at dusk is a dramatic visual experience also not to be missed (http://www.nps.gov/cave).

Some 40 miles to the south of Carlsbad over the Texas border is Guadalupe Mountains National Park. As its name suggests, the principal visual element of this park is mountains, and the park includes the highest peak in Texas—Guadalupe Peak at 8,749 feet—and the scenic stone face of El Capitan, which is at 8,085 feet the most southerly of the Guadalupe mountain peaks (Newhouse 1997). Mountains, however, are not the only visual attractions in this park. There are three other features available to

Fig. 4-9 Big Bend

hikers and horseback riders. The first is desert both on the east and west of the park featuring a variety of grasses, junipers, and pines. The second is canyon interiors, such as McKittrick Canyon, with maple, ash, and oak trees. Third, there are alpine uplands with Ponderosa and white pine, Douglas fir, and aspen (http://www.nps.gov). Although the peaks are not so high as they are in the Guadalupe Mountains, Big Bend National Park offers similar visual experiences for the visitor.

Big Bend National Park is remote even for a part of Texas that is already thinly populated. A drive into the park from the north, usually from the town of Marathon, is so desolate that the sighting of another vehicle or even an animal is rare. Travelers are warned, as they are at Death Valley and other similar remote national parks, to be sure they have sufficient water and fuel. However, the park itself is not really so desolate as it might seem at first view. It is a birder's paradise, with more than 450 species of birds to see at one time or another and more than at any other national park. After heavy rains, the park is also colorful and full of wildflowers. Hikers may also see quite a variety of animals, such as roadrunners, peccaries, coyotes, and kangaroo rats as well as some potentially dangerous mountain lions and Mexican black bears. Hikers should observe posted warnings carefully.

Fig. 4-10 Big Bend Santa Elena Canyon

For those visitors not wishing to or not able to engage in what are often strenuous hikes, Big Bend is quite accessible through the many roads throughout the park. The Chisos Mountains provide the visitor with upland scenery, trees, and the only lodging and food available in the park itself. The Chisos Basin is characteristically desert and has a variety of canyons and horseback and hiking trails. Santa Elena Canyon offers a dramatic view of the steep cliffs carved by the Rio Grande River as well as the calm vista of the river itself. At this point, the river is quite narrow and tranquil.

In the eastern US may be found two more national parks featuring mountains, although these mountains are quite different in appearance from the ones of the west. The parks are Shenandoah National Park and Great Smoky Mountains National Park. Shenandoah is a long, narrow park in the Blue Ridge Mountains of Virginia featuring a road, Skyline Drive, that courses the length of the park from north to south along a mountain ridge. Shenandoah is a favorite destination for campers and hikers, who find its many trails leading to numerous waterfalls challenging and visually rewarding routes. The mountains of the eastern US are not set in or even near deserts and are heavily forested wilderness areas. Not only do visitors come to Shenandoah for the stunning mountain vistas but also in the fall for the brilliant and colorful changing foliage. Commencing at the southern end of the park, the Blue Ridge Parkway takes the visitor quickly to nearby Great Smoky Mountains National Park on the borders of western Tennessee and eastern North Carolina.

Great Smoky Mountains National Park is visited by twice the number of people each year than any other national park (Newhouse 1997). Gatlinburg, Tennessee, at one of the park's northern entrances is a popular honeymoon destination for many couples. Like Shenandoah, the Great Smokies offer a vast wilderness accessible via automobile as well as numerous trails for hiking or just walking. They also attract visitors in the fall seeking the beauty of changing foliage. The highest point in the park, Clingman's Dome, offers spectacular views of the mountains and wilderness. Cades Cove is a high valley where one may well see many of the park's animal population, including black bear and white-tailed deer. At the extreme southern end of the state of Florida lies another of America's most unique national parks. It is the million and a half acre natural phenomenon of the Everglades.

Everglades National Park is a vast watery ecosystem of bays in the west, sloughs, channels, mangrove swamps, saw grass, and slash pine. Although certainly as green as any mountain wilderness, the swampy Everglades offer the ultimate contrast to mountains—flat surfaces as far as the eye can see. Visitors come to the park not only for its visual attractions but also for the many species of wildlife, including the American crocodile, the West Indian manatee, many types of wading birds, and the like (http://www.nps.gov).

Although this chapter is about US national parks, it is by no means the case that the US is the only nation which has officially designated national parks. By 2003, the United Nations had recognized 102,102 national parks and similar protected places worldwide (Runte 2010). The motivation for establishing such places remains the preservation of spectacular scenery and unique geological features, but there are other reasons as well. "Civilization is the problem parks solve" (Runte 2010, 238). As the world's population has grown to over seven billion, there is inevitable pressure to use land for human habitat rather than save it as a legacy. It is the case that throughout the world, some of the most spectacular visual experiences are still available for visitors to see.

In the United Kingdom, for example, there are Snowdonia National Park, Northumberland, Brecon Beacons, and Loch Lomond to name but a few, and in Ireland there are the Wicklow Mountains. In Europe, there are Calanques National Park in the south of France, Berchtesgaden National Park in southern Germany, the Cinque Terre in Italy, and the Sierra Nevada in Spain, again to name but a very few. There are national parks in Africa and Asia as well. In Australia, there is Port Campbell National Park, which includes the Great Ocean Road and the rock formations off the coast known as the Twelve Apostles southwest of Melbourne, and the

Fig. 4-11 Wicklow Mountains

Blue Mountains National Park west of Sydney. New Zealand features Tongariro National Park and Fiordland National Park. Simply as examples of national parks outside the US, the following parks will be considered for their visual effects: Wicklow Mountains, Calanques, Port Campbell, and the Blue Mountains.

Wicklow Mountains National Park south of Dublin stands as one of the very best examples of why Ireland is called the Emerald Isle. The Wicklow Mountains are actually only hills, but they are covered with the greenery of trees and grasses and sprinkled with lakes, streams, and peat bogs. Hillwalking along the many trails in the park is a popular visitor activity, but viewing the scenery is the park's principal attraction. Regular day tours from Dublin bring many visitors to the park, and movie crews have found the scenery to be good for many types of location shoots. The valley of Glendalough is the park's information center and the location of shops, restaurants, and the ruins of St. Kevin's monastic settlement of the 6th century.

Calanques National Park lies on the southern coast of France between Marseille and Cassis. A calanque is a cove or inlet formed between sheer rock faces usually of limestone. The panorama of white limestone rock

Fig. 4-12 Calanques

and azure sea draws many visitors to this comparatively new (opened in 2012) national park. Hiking and rock climbing are also popular activities, although the area is sometimes off limits for its fragility.

On the other side of the globe and in the southern hemisphere are two Australian national parks of note—Port Campbell National Park southwest of Melbourne and Blue Mountains National Park west of Sydney. The Great Ocean Road is a long, scenic drive along the Southern Ocean coast, which is a popular day tour out of Melbourne. Similar in many ways to the coastal drive of Highway 1 in California, there are beautiful ocean and hillside views along the Great Ocean Road. Perhaps the most visually spectacular, however, is the area off the coast in Port Campbell National Park featuring the Twelve Apostles. These are rock formations just off the coast itself formed by cliffside erosion. The name is somewhat misleading, since there were ever only nine limestone outcroppings. The erosion, unfortunately, is continuous, and there are now only eight distinct formations. On the other hand, there are a number of other similar formations worth seeing, including London Arch and Loch Ard gorge.

The Blue Mountains, west of Sydney, are similar to the American Shenandoah and Great Smoky Mountains National Parks but with gorges and sheer rock faces reminiscent of the canyon parks of the American west. The greenery includes both eucalyptus forest and, in the sheltered valleys, rainforest. There are waterfalls to be seen and caves to visit. Perhaps the most impressive visual sight is the rock formation called the Three Sisters, which is the result of erosion.

With national parks, as noted earlier, the space is not designed in the sense pleasure gardens and city parks are. This, however, does not make national parks any the less visually compelling. In fact, man-made outdoor

Fig. 4-13 Twelve Apostles

spaces mimic nature to a large extent. "No doubt about it. The first gardens were not made, but discovered. A natural spot—a clearing in the forest, a valley opening up in a barren mountain-side, an island in a remote lake—made pleasant by a belt of trees, flowering, fragrant, and bearing fruit. . . . In the oldest accounts, such spots are the gardens of the gods, or of those favoured by the gods" (Thacker 1979, 9). The idea of such a "sacred grove" clearly lies at the heart of the US and other national park systems, where natural spots are set apart and preserved for all to see. Virtually any visitor to a national park can give a fair account of the visual impact of his or her visit. After all, it is primarily the visual experience for which visitors come to the national parks. From the point of view of this book, however, what is it that underlies this compelling visual experience? Why are national parks visually persuasive?

Perhaps the first answer to these questions has to do not with visual elements but with uniqueness. Wilderness, desert, giant trees, petrified trees, canyons, sheer rock faces, unusual rock formations, mountains, caverns, water, and swamp are the reasons for setting aside national parks in the first place, and were these features commonplace there would be no reason to do so. Coincident with uniqueness is, of course, preservation. However, there are visual elements underlying these unique natural

Fig. 4-14 Blue Mountains Three Sisters

phenomena that are shared with buildings and gardens and which explain their visual impact. In most cases, the first visual element of note is scale. The vast panorama of the Grand Canyon, the expanse of the Everglades, and the breadth of the Blue Mountains are the visual features that account primarily for the visitor's response. To some extent, mass is a part of scale, and that is particularly so in the case of rock faces, peaks, and rock formations. Color is an essential visual feature as well. The green of forested hills and mountains, of swamps, and of vast lawns cannot be ignored for its impact nor can the changing colors of leaves with the seasons. Light goes with color, but light can also be transformative in and of itself as it is in the dramatic effect of the rising sun at a place like Bryce Canyon. Line, both vertical and horizontal, commands the focus and movement of the eye as it observes natural phenomena, and different textures abound in wooded areas as well as swamps. In the next chapter, the subject is zoos and amusement parks, both of which are specialized examples of spaces designed for specific visual impacts on visitors.

Chapter Five

Zoological Gardens and Amusement Parks

J. Donald Ragsdale and Frances E. Brandau-Brown

Zoological gardens and amusement parks are specialized examples of the general idea of city parks. Although they serve several different purposes, such as the preservation of endangered species of animals and education in zoology itself, zoological gardens would hardly have survived and become so popular were it not for their entertainment function, particularly for children. They offer facilities and attractions enough to occupy a family for an entire day's outing if desired, whereas one would not normally think of an entire day spent in a city park. Where wildlife is the principal attraction in a zoological garden, it is the ride that is the attraction in an amusement park: a roller coaster, a Ferris wheel, or a carousel. Like zoological gardens, amusement parks offer sufficient facilities and attractions to occupy a family for a day or, in many cases now, more, with entertainment for children the principal focus. Indeed, the largest amusement park in the world, Walt Disney World in Orlando, Florida, is actually a resort complete with on-site hotels, golf courses, restaurants, and live entertainment, as well as the ubiquitous rides that could occupy visitors for multiple days. Amusement parks, and especially theme parks, use designed space to create a rather complete illusion of having left the real world and entered into a fantasy world of entertainment. It is not surprising, then, that part of Disney World is called the Magic Kingdom.

Zoological Gardens

Zoological gardens or, simply, zoos are directly connected to the pleasure gardens discussed in Chapter Two, such that the concepts underlying the visual power of pleasure gardens are the same for zoos. The development of the modern zoo took many of the same paths as did the gardens, although the origin of collecting animals, whether domestic or exotic, was quite different. Let us see how zoos began and how the idea of a zoo eventually merged with that of the pleasure garden. The history of zoos has been admirably recounted by Eric Baratay and Elisabeth Hardouin-Fugier in their fully illustrated volume *Zoo: A History of Zoological Gardens in the West* (2002), and the reader should refer to this book for a more complete account than the schematic one offered here. Similarly, the reader may wish to consult *Zoos and Tourism: Conservation, Education, Entertainment?* (Frost 2011) for a number of essays on the role of zoos in contemporary society and particularly as forms of entertainment. It should also be noted at this juncture that the idea of a zoo shares many features with the idea of a museum, which features will be briefly recounted here.

The idea of a collection of animals, especially wild ones, dates at least to the fifth and fourth millennia BCE in Egypt. The Egyptians regarded certain animals as sacred and kept them near temples. Cheetahs and lions were used to hunt in the second millennium and fostered a fascination with wild animals in general. In 14th century BCE China, wild animals were kept in imperial palaces. Similar practices were carried out in Assyria and Persia. The ancient Greeks did not develop seraglios, as they were called, until the time of Alexander the Great, although birds and monkeys were kept in some residences. The possession of tigers and elephants by Alexander and his successors was a symbol of power. In ancient Rome, the possession of aviaries, fish ponds, and caged animals symbolized wealth. However, the Romans also captured such animals as elephants, lions, and tigers during military expeditions and slaughtered them in the streets of Rome as a demonstration of military power. The collecting of wild as well as domestic animals to symbolize status or power continued through medieval times and the Renaissance (Baratay and Hardouin-Fugier 2002).

There was an explosion of interest in animal collections during the 15th and 16th centuries, largely due to reports of previously unknown animals by early explorers and traders. Some of these explorers also returned from their travels with specimens, both living and dead, of exotic animals and, for that matter, plants as well. Exotic plants found their way into many of the pleasure gardens of the aristocracy and royalty. Some explorers, like Christopher Columbus, even brought back human specimens of American Indians, dark skinned people, pygmies, and other human curiosities. The European aristocracy was especially important at this juncture, since it was not only interested in animals but also able to pay for them and for the expeditions needed to acquire them. It seemed natural to think of adding animal species as well as plants to pleasure gardens, and indeed most royals had hunting grounds already stocked with game animals such as deer and a variety of birds (Baratay and Hardouin-Fugier 2002).

European royalty in general were great collectors of art, and these collections provided pleasure to their owners and their guests as well as evidence of the wealth and power of the king or queen. So too did the pleasure gardens of royalty as noted in Chapter Two. For whatever pleasure these possessions afforded, it is important to emphasize for the present purposes the clear persuasive intent to establish prestige. It was no large leap at all to add an animal collection as evidence of royal prestige. Louis XIV became the person to imitate here as he was with the construction of Versailles and its gardens. About 1661, Louis built a seraglio of animals at the castle of Vincennes east of Paris and had them fight each other for the entertainment of his guests. "In 1662-4, Louis established a menagerie at Versailles, reserving it for exotic, rare and curious creatures. This particular enterprise marked a decisive step in the creation of menageries of curiosities and was imitated to some extent throughout Europe" (Baratay and Hardouin-Fugier 2002, 40). Eventually, the animal fights at Vincennes were ended and the animals incorporated into the menagerie at Versailles.

Louis permitted the public to view the grounds and the menagerie at Versailles as did the keepers of similar pleasure gardens throughout Europe. Gradually, cities began to support what can only be described as precursors of today's public zoological gardens. However, the origin of today's zoo probably lies in Louis XIV's menagerie, which fell into disrepair following Louis' death. By the time of the Revolution in 1789, the whole idea of a palace, a pleasure garden, and a menagerie fell into disfavor as a symbol of royalty, repression, and excess. Some of Louis' animals were destroyed, but eventually many of them were transferred to the French government's Jardin des Plantes, formerly the Jardin du Roi, in Paris. The construction of places to keep these animals marks the first actual zoo as it is known today. A small zoo remains at the Jardin des Plantes today. "The example of the Jardin des Plantes was followed throughout Europe thanks in part to the contemporary prestige of France, many of whose initiatives were more or less directly imposed, even in hostile countries and even after its own defeat. The spread of these influences strengthened and accelerated, and menageries came into being throughout Europe" (Baratay and Hardouin-Fugier 2002, 79).

The public was just as fascinated by exotic animals as had been the royalty and the aristocracy. A visit to the zoo became a formal outing with royalty appearing on Sundays and the public during the week. Traveling exhibits of animals and eventually circuses were also popular means of satisfying the curiosity of average citizens, much like traveling theatre companies. Quickly, private organizations were created to finance and control newly emerging zoological gardens and aquariums. While scientific research on the animals was a significant part of these enterprises, entertainment value, especially for children, was and remains the driving force (Baratay and Hardouin-Fugier 2002). With respect to children, the author lived for many years in Baton Rouge, LA, and taught at Louisiana State University. One of the local TV stations had two popular children's programs hosted by "Buckskin Bill" Black, who ended his shows each day with the remark "Remember, Baton Rouge needs a zoo." Bill's continuous refrain resulted eventually in Baton Rouge having a zoo, where collections of pennies from Bill's viewers and guests—he had a live audience as well—substantially defrayed the cost of the zoo's first pair of elephants. One was named Penny! There are probably other examples of such influences on the part of children.

Early enclosures for zoo animals were quite primitive, especially for fierce or dangerous animals. Even for relatively harmless species, fenced enclosures were the norm as they are today, and such animals as gorillas, orangutans, chimpanzees, lions, tigers, and other large cats were often contained in glass enclosures. Bear pits were common. As a concern for the welfare of zoo animals increased, some of these enclosures began to give way to those which simulated natural habitat and allowed animals much more space to roam. Safari parks, which allow visitors to drive through areas of free-roaming animals, are the natural extensions of these efforts to make the lives of captive animals more normal.

Concerns for animals' perceived freedom led directly to the most obvious aspect of visual persuasion in zoological gardens. As noted, efforts were made to create enclosures which simulated animals' natural habitat. Large ponds, for example, were created for such aquatic animals as seals and otters as well as for bears. Open grassy areas were built for lions, tigers, panthers, and cheetahs. Hills were built for mountain goats and similar species. In aquariums, enclosures with glass walls for viewing were made, so that alligators, snakes, turtles, and frogs could be seen both in and out of water. While the driving force for these changes in zoos was animal welfare, the result was an illusion for the visitor of having visited the actual lands where the animals originated, a visual experience akin to that of visiting such natural landscapes as there are to be found in national parks. However, there is another significant visual aspect of zoos that seems to be the result of the heritage of zoos as originally part of royal and aristocratic pleasure gardens.

Fig. 5-1 Berlin Zoo (Elephant Gate)

One does not merely go to a zoo or an aquarium to see animals. Instead, a zoo visit is analogous if not to a national park visit then to a city park outing. Relaxation, recreation, entertainment, and recuperation are all part of the reasons people visit zoos. Accordingly, zoos provide grounds other than the ones where animals are displayed that have landscape designs like city parks, with abundant plants and water features. Along with these outer grounds, if you will, there are refreshment stands and picnic areas to accommodate a variety of activities other than viewing the animals. Throughout zoos there is considerable attention paid to providing the visitor an unforgettable visual experience going beyond that of seeing the animals as will be seen in the ensuing pages.

Although there are many of them located throughout the world, the differences between zoos insofar as their visual persuasiveness is concerned are few. For that reason, only a small number of zoos will be considered here. The significant differences among zoos have to do with the animals in their collections, but the animals themselves are not the focus in this chapter. One of the most interesting examples of a zoo as a visually compelling designed space is Berlin's Zoologischer Garten. In most ways, this institution is the very prototype of a modern zoo and illustrates many aspects of the brief history presented here.

The Berlin Zoo is located at the southwestern corner of the Tiergarten. The Tiergarten was once a private hunting enclosure for royalty in Berlin, so there was a tradition of game keeping that made the designation of an area for a menagerie quite reasonable and certainly one in keeping with similar events throughout Europe. The Berlin Zoo was Germany's first, having been established in 1844, and is today Europe's most visited zoo. It is home to more than 1,400 species, which is said to be the most complete collection of species in the world (http://www.berlin.de). It houses some 13,700 animals. The original collection came from the menagerie and pheasantry of Frederick William IV, King of Prussia.

Fig. 5-2 Berlin Zoo Giraffe Enclosure

Visually, the Berlin Zoo is like many of the world's other modern zoos. Many of the animals are housed in enclosures where the environment mimics that of the animals' original habitat, even though some of the structures in these environments are artificial. Mountain goats have hills and caves, elephants have open spaces and ponds, and there are wading and swimming areas for penguins and other aquatic birds. Unfortunately, some species, such as orangutans and lions, remain confined in glass cages. Nonetheless, the visual experience for the visitor is for the most part that of having visited animals in the wild. In addition to the care given to creating what is largely an illusion of original habitat, the Berlin Zoo has also been attentive to providing a pleasure garden for its visitors.

There are two main entrances to the Berlin Zoo, one of which is the large and ornate Elephant Gate. The other is the smaller, but also ornate, Lion Gate directly across from Zoo Station, a major U-Bahn and S-Bahn hub in the city. As one passes through the Elephant Gate, a broad pedestrian boulevard opens up leading to a fountain and flanked by benches. In the center of the boulevard, a grassy area is planted with brightly colored flowers. One might almost forget that this is a zoo, and of course there are refreshment stands nearby as well. The experience is visually satisfying and relaxing. The Berlin Zoo also houses a substantial aquarium. While this part of the zoo is certainly interesting, it is less developed as a visual experience than are many other aquariums around the world. Most of the exhibits are simple tanks of varying sizes.

Fig. 5-3 Dublin Zoo Tiger Habitat

Dublin Zoo is Ireland's largest zoo and dates to 1830. It attracts more than 1 million visitors per year and is Ireland's most popular family attraction (http://www.dublinzoo.ie). It is located in the vast Phoenix Park, and it is also a prototypical modern zoo. The zoo houses about 400 animals representing some 100 species. Although it is clearly set off from the rest of Phoenix Park, Dublin Zoo seems more a continuation of the English landscape garden than an anomaly. Just at the entrance, a pathway

Fig. 5-4 Dublin Zoo Orangutan Habitat

through the zoo opens to the left. Another path to the right leads to the Meerkat Restaurant and a coffee shop. On the left pathway, one immediately encounters a long, narrow lake along which is arranged the Asian Forests exhibit. Included here, for example, to the left of the walkway are Asian lions, Sumatran tigers, and Snow leopards. On small islands on the edge of the lake are Siamang gibbons, Spider monkeys, and ring-tailed lemurs. Not only do the animals have relative freedom within apparently natural habitat, but the pathway is decorated with what appear to be native plants to foster the illusion of a trip to an exotic locale.

Continuing along the pathway, the visitor encounters the Fringes of the Arctic, the African Savanna, the Gorilla Rain Forest, and Chimpanzee Island, which is located at the end of a second lake above the first one. The one unfortunate aspect of a natural habitat with freedom for zoo animals is that shy animals like gorillas are not often seen by visitors. The pathway continues around this lake and along the eastern side of the zoo to the Kaziranga Forest Trail, and the Reptile House. Between the western and eastern pathways is a café and an exhibit of Humboldt penguins. Like the Berlin Zoo, Dublin Zoo is a visually compelling experience. With only a modicum of imagination, the visitor can believe that he or she is actually in native habitat. When one tires of walking, there are readily available places to find snacks, a meal, or liquid refreshment and benches on which to rest.

As might be expected, the US is replete with zoos, such that many comparatively small cities, such as Baton Rouge, LA, have zoos that are often comparable in size and diversity of animals to those in larger cities. Perhaps the best known zoos in the US are the Smithsonian National Zoological Park in Washington, DC, and the San Diego Zoo in Southern California. The National Zoo, as it is most often called, is a 163 acre facility located in Rock Creek Park and dating to 1889. It contains 2,000 animals representing about 400 different species. The zoo is a member of the American Public Gardens Association and advertises its gardens as part of the attraction of a zoo visit, which is essential to the visual persuasiveness of a zoo. Indeed, this zoo was designed by Frederick Law Olmsted, the designer of New York's Central Park and Montreal's Mount Royal Park. It is essentially styled like an English landscape garden (http://nationalzoo.si.edu).

Whereas Dublin Zoo is laid out vertically, in that it is narrower than it is wide, National Zoo spreads out horizontally. From an entrance on Connecticut Avenue that is beautifully decorated with flower beds and stone lions, a broad path leads north and then east through the park with smaller paths leading off to different exhibits. The Giant Panda Exhibit, the most popular in the park, is to be found shortly after embarking on the main path. The exhibits include a simulated African Savanna, an American and an Asian Trail, and the indoor domed exhibit called Amazonia with a river and an aquarium. A visitors' center and refreshment stands provide the visitor with the amenities for a day in the park (http://national zoo.si.edu).

San Diego's Zoo is also located in a park, this one being Balboa Park. This park was originally a 1,400 acre mesa of largely scrub land donated in 1868 by the city's civic leaders (http://www.balboapark.org). Eventually, trees and a variety of flowering shrubs were planted to give the park its modern character. Today, Balboa Park boasts a large number of museums, performing arts venues, attractions for children, a large variety of gardens, and the San Diego Zoo. This zoo is particularly known for its pioneering work in the area of cageless exhibits and natural habitat for its animal population. It is home to some 4,000 animals representing 80 species. A large topiary elephant stands at the zoo's entrance, which leads to a park that is oval shaped with the usual pathways leading to the various animal exhibits. The pathways are lined with tropical plants giving the visitor the impression of being in a natural habitat and providing shade and the visual impressiveness of color.

On the western side of the San Diego Zoo are the Big Cat Trail, the Hippo Trail, the Kiwi Trail, the Monkey Trail, the Orangutan Trail, and the Tiger Trail. Just right of center in the zoo is Panda Canyon and the Asian Passage. On the northeastern edge of the zoo is the Northern Frontier with polar bears and other cold climate animals and below that is a very large exhibit called Elephant Odyssey. There are many places to shop and dine at the zoo as well as recreation facilities designed for children, such as a petting zoo and a miniature train. Guests who choose to may take double decker bus tours of the zoo. The zoo also operates the 1,800 acre San Diego Zoo Safari Park east of downtown San Diego in the San Pasqual Valley (http://www.sdzsafaripark.org).

Safari parks are zoos that offer the ultimate wildlife experience short of the animals' natural habitats. Much larger than conventional zoos, safari parks permit animals to roam free, or apparently so at least. Of course, there are fences to restrain dangerous animals, but the effect is that of taking a safari in some remote location. The San Diego Safari Park offers a surprising array of wildlife, including gorillas, zebras, lions, cheetahs, elephants, giraffes, and many others, all in large open spaces landscaped to resemble native habitats. Visitors may take jeep or bus tours, and there is even a zip line over a portion of the park for those who would like a unique view (http://www.sdzsafaripark.org). Both the San Diego Zoo and the Safari Park represent the best of animal freedom combined with visual presentation resembling natural habitat. Safari parks, although fewer in number than zoos, have proliferated in the last several decades, not only in the US but also throughout the world. Fossil Rim Wildlife Center in Glen Rose, Texas, compares favorably in size to San Diego Safari Park and offers the visitor the opportunity to drive through the center in his or her personal vehicle.

Amusement Parks

Amusement parks originated much later than zoos and probably evolved from the English fair of the 12th century (Adams 1991). Fairs, of course, with their entertainers, exhibitions, midways, and craft stands continue today in the form of county and state fairs held annually in permanent fairgrounds, and there are of course world's fairs held at widely spaced intervals. Like zoos, amusement parks are to some degree an extension of the basic idea of the pleasure gardens discussed in Chapter

Two. They provide a place of respite and relaxation for visitors isolated from the quotidian concerns of work and the city, but they add the dimension of special forms of entertainment particularly for children and young adults. Unlike zoos and safari parks, which seek to put the visitor as nearly as possible into native habitat, albeit simulated for the most part, amusement parks seek to transport visitors to fantasy worlds. This is especially true of theme parks, which synthesize imaginary locales as in the case of the Pirates of the Caribbean in Walt Disney World and the Wizarding World of Harry Potter in Universal Studios Orlando. Space prohibits an examination of a large variety of amusement parks as examples of compelling designed spaces, thus this chapter will center its efforts on three exemplary and historically significant parks. These are Tivoli Gardens in Copenhagen, Denmark, Walt Disney World, in Orlando, Florida, and Universal Studios Orlando.

Fig. 5-5 Tivoli Gardens Fountain

Tivoli Gardens in Copenhagen was the brainchild of Georg Carstensen. Carstensen obtained permission from the Danish king to open this amusement park in 1843 (http://www.tivoli.dk). Although not the only nor the oldest such park in Europe, Tivoli is notable for its exemplary style and influence on the character of subsequent amusement parks. Walt

Disney visited Tivoli prior to the construction of Disney Land in Anaheim, California, the first Disney amusement park, and is said to have been strongly influenced by the Danish attraction. A visitor to both parks would have no trouble seeing the resemblances. Originally, Tivoli was located outside the city of Copenhagen in the west, but today the city has expanded not only to include the park but substantial additional areas of commercial and residential establishments beyond it. Just west across the street from Tivoli is the city's main train station, and east of the park across another main traffic artery is city hall.

Fig. 5-6 Tivoli Gardens Pirate Ship

Not quite the resort that some subsequent amusement parks have become, Tivoli Gardens nonetheless epitomizes the amusement park as a visually compelling designed space created for the pleasure and relaxation of those seeking respite from the pace of city life. The park is fenced and gated and covers 82,717 square metres or what appears to be two full city blocks (http://www.tivoli.dk). Although it does not incorporate significant hotel space (the Nimb Hotel offers 14 rooms), Tivoli is bordered on the west by an area of many places to stay. To create the pleasure garden augmented by rides, Tivoli at this writing (2013) features 43 dining facilities ranging from casual ones such as Hotdog Corner all the way to elegant restaurants such as Nimb Brasserie and Wagamama. There are also 14 ice cream outlets and candy stores. Shopping is not neglected either, with 16 stores offering everything from Teddy bears to jewelry. The 27 rides are spread around the park in such a way that there are large open areas of lawn with benches for picnicking and simply resting as well as fountains and a variety of flower gardens. At night, a special feature of Tivoli Gardens emerges with the illumination of 120,000 light bulbs.

The 27 rides at Tivoli Gardens are for the most part traditional ones, including a roller coaster attraction that is currently celebrating its 100th anniversary of operation. There are also the Classic Carousel, the Trolley Car, the Galley Ships, the Dragon, and many more. In a sizable lake within the park, there is an anchored replica of a pirate ship housing a family restaurant. Twelve entertainment venues, ranging from the Pantomime Theatre to the Open Air Stage, complete the attractions offered for the visitor's pleasure. It is probably correct to see such amusement parks as Tivoli Gardens as children's attractions with enough adult-oriented features to keep an entire family entertained. However, it is also the case that adults without children visit the park for the pleasures it offers even without riding the rides much as they do in places such as Manhattan's Central Park.

Walt Disney World in Orlando, Florida, represents the zenith of amusement and theme park development. It is the world's largest resort, although not the only Disney theme park. The first Disney park, Disney Land, was built nearer Disney's Hollywood studios in Anaheim, California, and there are similar Disney theme parks just outside Paris, France, and in Tokyo, Hong Kong, and Shanghai. Envisioning this largest resort, Walt Disney bought some 40 square miles of largely unusable land near the small city of Orlando and transformed the acreage into a 25,000 acre resort, which includes four separate theme parks. Once on the outskirts of Orlando in Lake Buena Vista, today Disney World is virtually part of the expanding city (http://www.waltdisneyworld.com.

Within the confines of the Disney World resort, there are numerous resort hotels, which provide transportation to the various attractions available. There is also a well-traveled and state of the art monorail system to shuttle visitors to various spots within the resort. Additionally, there are a wide variety of restaurants catering to all kinds of tastes, and various venues throughout the park offer live entertainment during the day and early evening. The last feature of each day is an illumination show done with 1,000 separate fireworks.

The spiritual center of Disney World is the Magic Kingdom theme park. This part of the resort was the first to open, and it is the part of the

Fig. 5-7 Disney World Cinderella's Castle

resort most specifically connected to the well-known Disney animated cartoons. Actors dressed as Mickey Mouse, Minnie Mouse, Goofy, and other familiar characters roam the streets to greet visitors and have their pictures taken. Entering the Magic Kingdom, one first arrives at a near full scale version of Main Street USA. The buildings, indeed the entire designed space, are intended to usher the visitor from everyday reality into the down-home fantasy of small-town America. Then, Main Street itself is a designed space whose purpose is to funnel visitors toward the various rides and other attractions that are associated with Disney cartoon themes. At the end of Main Street is Cinderella's Castle, modeled after some of the actual castles of Europe, such as Neuschwanstein in Bavaria, which serves as the hub from which pathways to the rides and other attractions all radiate. Like Dreamland at Coney Island, New York, before it, Disney World "set an important tradition, namely . . . to actively control the flow and pacing of patrons at the park" (Lukas 2008, 62). The design of space to accomplish this control is so subtle as to be hardly noticeable by the visitor.

There are sufficient rides to keep visitors occupied for the most part of an entire day. Some of the best known of these are the Swiss Family Treehouse, Space Mountain, an enclosed roller coaster operating in the dark, the Pirates of the Caribbean boat ride, the Jungle Cruise, the Hall of Presidents, and the Big Thunder Mountain Railroad, also a roller coaster. Although one might find roller coasters and other such rides in any amusement park, the Disney World rides put the visitor into a simulated fantasy world that has all the appearances of reality. The Pirates of the Caribbean ride, for example, is so realistic that it has spawned a series of Hollywood movies based on the theme. Throughout the Magic Kingdom, there are in addition to the rides a large variety of concessions as well as benches and green spaces for resting.

Fig. 5-8 Epcot Center World Showcase

Somewhat more appealing to adult visitors to Disney World is the Epcot theme park, which is three times the size of the Magic Kingdom and the second to be built within the resort. Originally conceived of as an experimental city of the future, today's Epcot features two distinct aspects. Future World offers attractions having to do with technology and innovation and World Showcase has themed pavilions representing a number of other countries. There are also numerous small gardens and water features in Epcot. The theme park's entrance is dominated by Spaceship Earth, a gigantic geodesic dome and the heart of Future World, and the areas within the dome and nearby allow the visitor to experience technological innovations expected to be part of everyday life in the future. Some of these attractions include the Universe of Energy, Mission: SPACE, and the Land. Like the Magic Kingdom, the spaces are designed to simulate the future for the visitor.

World Showcase consists of eleven pavilions, reminiscent of a world's fair, which take the visitor into another country and are highly realistic. They do not merely represent the country but simulate the actual foreign environment complete with buildings that replicate those in the other culture. So, the visitor who has never left the US can feel as if he or she has actually been to France, Morocco, the UK, or Germany and actually enjoyed the local cuisine. The pavilions are staffed by international representatives. They are arranged in a circle around a large, man-made lagoon whose pathways subtly guide the visitor from one attraction to another.

Fig. 5-9 Disney World White Tigers

The third theme park in the Disney World Resort is Disney's Hollywood Studios. Unlike the other theme parks, Disney's Hollywood Studios omits the design feature of pathways which subtly lead the visitor from one area to another. This theme park is actually a working cinema studio, complete with stage sets where the visitor can immerse him or herself in the trappings of an actual movie production. The park also includes rides and live entertainment, however, and these are connected directly to the theme of Hollywood, show business, and cinema production. There are six areas of interest in Disney's Hollywood Studios. Hollywood Boulevard is the main entrance and is similar in form and function to Main Street in the Magic Kingdom. Echo Lake is a small lagoon and features rides themed to the *Star Wars* films. The Streets of America offers a studio backlot tour among other attractions. Animation Courtyard focuses on Disney animation production. Pixar Place offers insight into the *Toy Story* animation series. Last, Sunset Boulevard features the Hollywood Tower Hotel, which has the theme of a haunted elevator, and an elaborate, live auto stunt show.

Finally, Disney World features a fourth theme park that is actually a highly structured and controlled zoological garden called Disney's Animal Kingdom. It is five times the size of the Magic Kingdom and was originally a cow pasture. Four million plants were planted here to transform the pasture into a visually convincing African savanna. It offers the visitor a 100 acre safari ride in an open tram, which on the face of it would seem quite dangerous given the number of wild animals on view. However, the ride is an illusion. The park is designed with hidden berms and other barriers which keep animals like lions and tigers separated from giraffes and zebras and the like as well as from the park's patrons. Like other zoos, the Animal Kingdom focuses on species preservation, but it takes the experience of wildlife and wildlife habitat to its utmost lengths. Like the rest of Walt Disney World, the Animal Kingdom immerses the visitor in a simulated world which makes fantasy seem to be real. Lukas (2008, 22) alludes to this apotheosis of theme parks as "powerful forms of artificiality that challenged the real and provided a refuge or oasis in contrast with the chaos of the outside world."

Universal Studios Orlando is one of several amusement parks developed in Orlando evidently seeking to capitalize on the large number of visitors to Disney World. Along with such other attractions as Sea World and innumerable smaller water parks, Universal Studios Orlando is a large, resort style amusement park rivaling its cross-town competitor. Before the development of Disney World, Orlando was a small town characterized by swamp land and orange groves. As the number of visitors to Disney World grew in size, the city itself also expanded. Principally, resorts, hotels, and motels began to dot the landscape, and these were followed by the construction of interstate highways. Today's visitor to Orlando has a large variety of attractions in which to spend time while away from the theme parks and water parks, such as shopping malls, cinemas, reduced price outlet malls, a vast array of restaurants, and the like.

As its name suggests, Universal Studios Orlando, like Disney's Hollywood Studios, is themed around cinema production and especially rides, attractions, and entertainment that have to do with actual films (http://www.universalorlando.com). It advertises its rides as *"thrilling—* thus distinguishing itself from Disney parks, which offer nothing more than 'Yesterday's Classic Fairytales'" (Lukas 2008, 89). There are two sections to the theme park. Universal Studios Florida includes an active cinema production studio and rides based on such films as *Transformers, Despicable Me, Shrek, Beetlejuice,* and *The Blues Brothers.* Islands of Adventure offers rides based on films like *Jurassic Park, The Cat in the Hat, The Incredible Hulk,* and *Spiderman.* It also now gives the visitor the chance to enter into the world of the Harry Potter books and movies with The Wizarding World of Harry Potter. "Universal Studios Florida asks patrons to step inside conceptual spaces—ones that have already been reworked through the multiple permutations of motion pictures" (Lukas 2008, 90). Universal Studios Orlando, like Disney World, offers the visitor a complete experience in that there are a number of on-site hotels and restaurants as well as permanent installations of live entertainment such as that of the Blue Man Group.

Zoological gardens and amusement or theme parks evolved out of and are based on most of the same premises as the great pleasure gardens of Europe. City parks and the designation of unusual land areas as national parks also evolved in this way. Zoos and theme parks, however, do not merely offer respite and relaxation. They are not only oases, but rather they typify the use of designed space to permit something akin to transformation into another realm. "Like our early human ancestors who may have used symbolic caves to deal with the unrealities, the difficulties, of the real world, we use these virtual spaces to do much the same. . . . the theme park, like the utilitarian and symbolic forms of the past, provides people across the world with a way out of life and a uniquely new way of life" (Lukas 2008, 244-245).

CHAPTER SIX

HALLOWED GROUND:
BATTLEFIELDS, CEMETERIES, AND MONUMENTS

Countries around the world have chosen to regard battlefields as hallowed ground and have preserved many of these sites as places of remembrance. Sometimes cemeteries adjoin these battlefields, while in other cases battlefield dead are interred in nearby areas. In both battlefields and cemeteries, and occasionally standing alone, countries have also built monuments to honor those who died in battle. Elsewhere, the author has likened such designed spaces to an ancient form of oratory called epideictic (Ragsdale 2007). Epideictic oratory, unlike that found in law courts or legislative assemblies, "was the rhetoric of praise or blame, often to be heard in funeral orations. One took to the podium either to magnify the memory of a dead hero or to excoriate the reputation of a foe" (102). Of the few surviving accounts of oratory from the ancient world, Pericles Funeral Oration exemplifies an epideictic speech honoring Greek warriors who fell in battle.

There were four types of epideictic: panegyric, encomium, the funeral oration, and invective. A panegyric was a flamboyant speech of praise of the sort one might hear at a festival or, in our time, at a political convention. Encomiums were also speeches of praise, but they were less elaborate than panegyrics and usually were directed at a single person. An encomium would likely be heard at a banquet for a retiring employee. Although spectacular funeral orations have largely passed from the scene, today's funerals often contain one or more eulogies offered in praise of the deceased. Invective is a speech of blame, often a vituperative personal attack, and may have been much less common in the ancient world than the other three forms of epideictic. Today, invective may be confined to the world of politics and may best be seen in mudslinging attacks on an opponent.

How are designed spaces like these forms of epideictic oratory? Monuments and their locations are often like panegyrics or encomiums in that they serve as instruments of praise. The Arc de Triomphe in Paris is like a panegyric in the flamboyance of its praise, and the many monuments to such men as Franklin D. Roosevelt and Abraham Lincoln in Washington, DC, are like encomiums. In the case of eulogies, cemetery stones offer abundant tributes to the deceased. In a larger sense, hallowed ground itself is a testament to those whose lives were lost in battle. As will be seen, sometimes the ruins of war are left as they are as if to cry out against the evil that descended upon them, in which case the location is analogous to invective. This analogy to the ancient oratory of epideictic will prove useful in understanding the designed spaces of hallowed ground.

There are three major types of hallowed ground. In many cases, spaces have been preserved and decorated with monuments, statues, and such relics of war as cannons and cannonballs. The motivation is not merely to satisfy the curious visitor but to offer an object lesson in the horror of war, so that the visitor does not forget. In other cases, spaces are set aside as memorials and cemeteries near, but not necessarily on, the site of a battlefield. Whereas the first type is a preserved battlefield left to resemble its appearance at the time of war, the second type is a carefully designed and implemented memorial to the dead. A third type shares some of the characteristics of the first two but is distinguished by its singular and usually freestanding nature. It is a monument, which to be sure may be found in battlefields and cemeteries. However, there are occasions where monuments alone commemorate a war event, and normally these monuments are surrounded by carefully designed if small spaces.

The first type of hallowed ground, which will be called a preserved battlefield, includes in France such places as the Verdun Battlefield of World War II, the remains of the village of Oradour-sur-Glane near Limoges, and in Berlin, Germany, the remains of the Kaiser-Wilhelm-Gedächtniskirche. In the US, there are the several Civil War battlefield sites, notably the ones at Gettysburg in Pennsylvania, Manassas Bull Run in Virginia, Chickamauga in Georgia, and Vicksburg in Mississippi. In Texas, there is the San Jacinto Battleground State Historic Site commemorating the victory of Sam Houston and his band of "Texians" over Santa Anna's larger Mexican force and the resulting independence of Texas. Then, there is the Little Bighorn Battlefield National Monument in Montana, site of General George A. Custer's so-called Last Stand. These sites, and others like them, permit visitors to view spaces of battle and to imagine the way events actually unfolded unimpeded by alterations to the landscape.

The second type, which will be called a battlefield memorial and cemetery, has a somewhat different purpose in that it is less concerned with a visitor's ability to imagine a battle and more interested in designing a space in which the dead can be honored and the visitor given an opportunity to reflect in tranquility. The United States is fortunate indeed never to have had to fight a foreign aggressor on its own soil after the War of 1812. As a result, there are very few battlefield memorials and cemeteries in the US. On the other hand, there are a surprising number of American battlefield memorials and cemeteries in locations outside the United States, which commemorate battles of World Wars I and II. Indeed, there is an official American Battle Monuments Commission whose responsibility it is to oversee and maintain 24 overseas military cemeteries where nearly 125,000 fallen American servicemen and women are interred (http://www.abmc.gov).

The Commission is also responsible for 25 memorials, monuments, and markers around the world, and these constitute the third type of place of remembrance. What is distinctive for the purposes of this book about these American battlefield memorials, cemeteries, and monuments is not just that they are battle sites and burial grounds but that they are also clearly parks and gardens in the same sense that pleasure gardens, landscape gardens, city parks, and the like are and that they are thought of as visitor destinations in almost the same way. The ABMC website (http://www.abmc.gov) features a video entitled "Fields of Honor," which says of the cemeteries that "each is a masterpiece of landscape design" and not only a resting place for the fallen but "also intended for the living." For these reasons, the memorials and cemeteries especially have landscape designs that rival locations assessed in previous chapters of this book.

One does not only visit a battlefield memorial and cemetery to seek the grave of a relative or loved one but also to confront preserved history and honor the sacrifices of the dead. Clearly, the dead might merely have been interred without any consideration for visual impact but tellingly they have not been. A designed space has been thought of as an essential accompaniment to the graves themselves. Not only does the visitor see the cemeteries proper but ponds, fountains, reflecting pools, sculpted trees and shrubs, profusions of blooming plants, sculpture, and art among other things. In this chapter, several ABMC battlefield cemeteries and memorials will be examined for their visual impact. Arguably, the best known of these is the Normandy American Cemetery in France on a bluff overlooking the landing beaches of World War II's D-Day, but there are others to be found in England, Belgium, Italy, North Africa, and the Philippines, as well as Mexico and Hawaii. Finally, the chapter will consider several of the ABMC free-standing monuments scattered throughout the world. Although the preserved battlefield is not so clearly a designed space as the battlefield memorial and cemetery, it offers a useful point of departure for assessment in this chapter.

Preserved Battlefields

Fig. 6-1 Verdun Shell Marked Battlefield

Outside the small village of Verdun in northeastern France, German forces in World War I began the longest battle of the war on February 21, 1916. It lasted for 300 days and resulted in the loss of perhaps 700,000 lives. For some perspective on it, this number exceeds the casualties on both sides in the American Civil War. The Verdun area was heavily fortified and a source of much French pride, such that German military leaders believed that French forces would fight there to the last man. Had that been the case, France would have indeed been unable to continue armed resistance to the Germans. Seeking this devastating outcome, the German army launched some 2,500,000 shells from 1,200 artillery guns. The Germans took many French prisoners and occupied two of the major forts in the area, but an attack by British soldiers on the nearby area of the Somme drew German forces away from Verdun allowing it to be reclaimed by the French (http://www.historylearningsite.co.uk).

Two-thirds of the French army fought at Verdun, meaning that most French families were affected in one way or another by the battle. It is quite appropriate, therefore, that a memorial has been established at this battlefield (http://www.memorialdeverdun.fr). The site is hilly, and roads through it permit the visitor to see most of the important aspects of the memorial from a vehicle. There is a vast cemetery ringed by trees and shrubs around its perimeter, along with a memorial building and ossuary. What is visually striking about Verdun, however, is that the hills and trenches have been left as they were, so that the grounds are literally covered with shell holes from the massive German bombardment. Today of course, grass has grown to cover the bare ground, but the damage remains as mute testimony to this devastating battle. The effect on the viewer is quite clearly like that of invective on the listener. The preserved battlefield cries out against the horror of the events which took place at Verdun in 1916.

Fig. 6-2 Oradour sur Glane

Leaving the landscape as it was is a characteristic of preserved battlefields, although not all are so clearly marked as is Verdun. In what is perhaps an even more striking example of this practice is a village in central France, Oradour-sur-Glane, which is not actually even a battlefield. Instead, it is a place shelled almost to oblivion on June 10, 1944, by a detachment of Waffen-SS soldiers in World War II probably in retaliation for German losses on D-Day. The victims lie buried in a nearby cemetery, but the ruins have been left almost entirely alone. Half destroyed buildings and vehicles remain just as the shelling left them, and the site is now walled off as a memorial. The site is so visually striking that hardly any visitor speaks above a whisper. A sign at the entrance to the ruin reads "*Souviens-Toi*" (Remember). The visitor hardly needs the injunction.

Germany was, of course, eventually bombed extensively by squadrons of Allied airplanes, and this bombardment was carried not only to industrial centers but also to major city centers. Even Berlin was left in rubble. The rebuilding of West Germany and especially West Berlin constitutes one of the miracles of modern industry and economic growth, but in putting Berlin back together the German leaders seem to have had at least two guiding principles in mind. The first was not to rebuild structures clearly associated with the Third Reich, while the second was to leave some evidence remaining as a reminder of the vast destruction brought upon the city by Allied bombing. The Kaiser-Wilhelm-Gedächtniskirche in West Berlin was left a hollow shell by Allied bombing. There was little left of the building but a damaged spire. Although a new church was built adjacent to the ruins of the old, the ruin was left to stand as a reminder of the war's horror, and a memorial has been added on the ground floor.

Fig. 6-3 Kaiser-Wilhelm-Gedächtniskirche

In a vein similar to Verdun, Oradour, and the Kaiser Wilhelm Memorial Church, the Arizona Memorial in Pearl Harbor, Honolulu, Hawaii, is a preserved battlefield. The USS Arizona was one of the American battleships lost in the Japanese air attack on Pearl Harbor, December 7, 1941. Although some of the Arizona's sailors escaped, the great majority lost their lives when the vessel sank on its moorings in the harbor. Today, much of the vessel remains visible just below and in some cases above the surface of the harbor, and a memorial building has been erected over it to honor the Arizona's lost sailors as well as others whose lives were lost that day. The Arizona was simply left as it was and even now continues to leak oil from its holds. The sight, especially in the counterpoint of the beautiful surroundings of Pearl Harbor and the lush greenery of the shore, is visually dramatic and emotionally draining. Places like Verdun, Oradour, the Kaiser Wilhelm Church, and the Arizona site in Pearl Harbor are all like the oratory of invective. They cry out against the horror of war.

American battlefields of the Civil War do not present the obvious scars of battle as those discussed above, but they have been preserved as much as possible in their wartime state so as to allow the visitor to see the terrain and imagine the battle. Gettysburg National Military Park in Pennsylvania is probably the best known of these preserved battlefields. Perhaps because of the fame of Abraham Lincoln's Gettysburg Address, the battle of Gettysburg is known to virtually every American school boy and girl. However, there is much more to the battle that marks this place as hallowed ground. Confederate General Robert E. Lee had led his troops into the North before, but the ensuing battle at Antietam in Maryland had ended in a draw. Flush with the success of the Confederate forces at Chancellorsville, Virginia, a month before, Lee led his men into Pennsylvania, with plans to win the decisive victory that would turn the war against the North. The battle lasted three days, from July 1 to July 3, 1863, and was indeed the turning point of the war. Unfortunately for the Confederates, Lee's army was defeated by General George Meade's Army of the Potomac. The Confederates retreated on July 4, 1863, and on that same day Vicksburg fell to Union forces in the western theater of the war (Vandiver 2002). The areas of battle at Gettysburg today remain as open fields and hills with both wooden and stone fence lines marking major sites. The park is also sprinkled with monuments to the various troops that fought there, along with cannon and statues. It is the 150th anniversary of the battle at this writing, and hundreds of visitors are reported to have come to Gettysburg to witness historical reenactments of the battles.

Preserved battlefields like Manassas Bull Run in northern Virginia, Chickamauga in northwestern Georgia, and Vicksburg in Mississippi follow the pattern of Gettysburg in terms of their layouts and the monuments, cannon, and statues that have been placed there. Some also have houses and small buildings remaining from the period of the war. At Vicksburg National Military Park, forts and trenches have been reconstructed to enhance the visual presentation, and this hilly site is covered with monuments. There were two Civil War battles at Manassas, Virginia, and the creek called Bull Run. The first began on July 21, 1861, and resulted in a Confederate victory. The second was a year later on August 29-30, 1862. In both battles, Union forces attacked Confederate troops and were repulsed. Victory in the second battle paved the way for General Lee's first invasion of the North at Antietam (Vandiver 2002).

Union troops under the command of General William S. Rosecrans attacked Chattanooga, Tennessee, forcing Confederate forces under General Braxton Bragg to evacuate to Chickamauga, Georgia. From Chickamauga on September 19-20, 1863, the Confederates counterattacked and forced the Union side back into Chattanooga. This battle, however, was especially costly for the Confederates who lost some 18,000 of their forces. Two months later the Union army won decisively at Chattanooga, Tennessee, which became the base for Northern expeditions into Georgia and Alabama. Perhaps the greatest Union success of the war was at Vicksburg in Mississippi. The end of a 47 day siege of the city by Generals U. S. Grant and William T. Sherman on July 4, 1863, effectively divided the Confederacy and gave Union troops control of the vital Mississippi River (Vandiver 2002).

Much like these Civil War preserved battlefields, the San Jacinto Battleground State Historic Site in La Porte, Texas, and the Little Bighorn Battlefield in Montana stand as stark visual reminders of the end of the Texas war for independence from Mexico and the so-called last stand of General George A. Custer against an overwhelming Native American force. Most Americans are familiar with the massacre in March, 1836, at the Alamo in San Antonio and the battle cry "Remember the Alamo." Less well-known is the Battle of San Jacinto, where General Sam Houston and a small band of Texian soldiers, as they were called, surprised the larger Mexican force of General Santa Anna and defeated them on April 21, 1836. Today, a tall monument facing a reflecting pool commemorates this most important date in Texas history. The marshy, coastal area of the site hardly resembles a battlefield.

By contrast, the arid and dusty hills of southeastern Montana all too clearly resemble a battlefield. Aside from a walkway with explanatory markers and a small cemetery, the hills and ravines of the Little Bighorn Battlefield, left as they were in June of 1876, are a stark visual reminder of the conditions the Custer Battalion of the US Army's Seventh Cavalry faced when encircled by Lakota and Northern Cheyenne warriors. One is struck by the lack of any place to retreat or to hide and by the ease with which the cavalry could be attacked from ambush. Where preserved battlefields permit the visitor to imagine the actual battles they memorialize, they are not quite the designed spaces that battlefield memorials and cemeteries are. As will be seen, the American Battle Monuments Commission (ABMC) has gone to great lengths to insure that US military personnel who are interred abroad and near the places where they fell rest in locations that are every bit the equal of the great city parks discussed in Chapter Three. The Commission's website features short video tours of every battle monument, which is the source of much of the description and facts which follow (http://www.abmc.gov).

Battlefield Memorials and Cemeteries

Many of the ABMC battlefield memorials and cemeteries in Europe are the hallowed ground of World War I. The largest of these is the Meuse-Argonne American Cemetery and Memorial in France 26 miles northwest of Verdun. It covers 130.5 acres and contains the graves of 14,246 American service personnel. A memorial chapel stands on a ridge overlooking the cemetery and a tree lined lawn leading to a pond and flower beds. The cemetery consists of eight plots, each of which is ringed by sculpted trees. As will be seen, the ABMC memorials and cemeteries share many of these design features.

Aisne-Marne American Cemetery and Memorial is located near the village of Belleau and a short distance northwest of Château-Thierry. Its 42.5 acres contain the remains of 2,289 service personnel most of whom lost their lives in fighting during the summer of 1918. The cemetery is lined with trees alternating in size. The entrance gate leads to a flower and tree lined avenue to a memorial chapel. There are trenches and weapons remaining at nearby Belleau Wood. The garden features of flower beds, sculpted shrubs and trees, meticulously tended green lawns, and the occasional pond are common to most of these memorial cemetery sites.

Of course, western Europe is also liberally sprinkled with ABMC memorials and cemeteries from US involvement in World War II. Undoubtedly the most famous of all the American battlefield memorials and cemeteries is the one in Normandy, France, overlooking the landing beaches of D-Day, which on June 6, 1944, marked the Allied invasion of France and the beginning of the end of the Nazi war machine. The beaches themselves no longer bear the scars of war, but looking down at them from the hills above and out over the English Channel makes the many photographic images and movie reenactments come easily to life. The hills themselves, however, still have the concrete bunkers from which German artillery fired on the landing craft on D-Day. Just back of the view of the

Fig. 6-4 Normandy American Cemetery

beaches is the American cemetery. In the case of all of the ABMC sites, the cemetery is one of the most visually striking features. There are 9,387 graves here, all laid out in symmetrical rows and columns with each one marked by a small white cross. As in Arlington National Cemetery outside Washington, DC, the cemetery itself is a poignant reminder of how many American lives were lost. The grid layout of the cemetery suggests the rank and file of a marching army.

The cemetery at Normandy also has a large memorial in the form of two semicircular colonnades in the middle of which is a large bronze statue called the "Spirit of American Youth" fronted by a reflecting pool. There is also a small, circular, colonnaded chapel on the grounds. The grounds are adorned with a number of plots of flowering plants, and the burial plots are bounded by both trees and shrubs, many of which are sculpted into topiaries in the form of cones, rectangles, and trapezoids. Obviously, great and continuing care has been put into maintaining the Normandy cemetery as a type of landscape garden fit not only to memorialize the dead but also to reassure the living.

Not far away is Brittany American Cemetery and Memorial with 28 acres and 4,410 graves where many other service personnel who participated in the Normandy invasions and the early battles in northwestern France are interred. There is a Romanesque chapel here, and

Fig. 6-5 Normandy "Spirit of American Youth"

the burial plots are framed by trees and accented by flower gardens. It is always a somber occasion to visit such a place, but the ABMC has made sure that it has landscape designs which honor the dead by their precision and color.

Much of the fighting after D-Day occurred in northeastern France as the Allies advanced toward the Rhine. Two American cemeteries and memorials, one at Epinal and the other in Lorraine, are the final resting places of many of those who lost their lives in this offensive. Epinal's 48.6 acres lie 100 feet above the Moselle River in the Vosges Mountains and have 5,255 graves. There is a rectangular memorial building here fronting an open lawn bounded on either side by a double row of sculpted trees. The burial plots lie on either side of these rows of trees. The largest World War II cemetery in Europe is at Lorraine. Here there are 10,489 graves in nine elliptically arranged plots.

One of the most important battles of World War II, and the last major counterattack by the Germans, was the Battle of the Bulge in Belgium. The Ardennes American Cemetery and Memorial, which contains the graves of many of the soldiers who were killed in this battle, is 12 miles south of Liège and covers 90 acres containing 5,323 burial plots. The graves form a Greek cross and are framed by trees. There is the rather ubiquitous memorial building and a bronze statue representing youth, although this memorial is more massive than most and features a huge carved American eagle.

Major battles of World War II took place all along the length of Italy. Outside Florence, there is a 70 acre cemetery where lie 4,402 service personnel who lost their lives in the fighting around Rome. Here, too, is a memorial structure, this one in the shape of a pylon, facing a lawn like avenue lined with double rows of trees with the burial plots on either side. World War II in the Pacific, by comparison to the effort in Europe, has only one ABMC site. This one is in Manila in the Philippines.

The Manila American Cemetery and Memorial is the largest of all the cemeteries of World War II and contains the graves of 17,201 service personnel who died in the Philippines and New Guinea. It covers 152 acres on a high plateau easily visible from almost all directions of the compass. Here there are 11 burial plots in a generally circular plan and carefully landscaped with a variety of tropical plants and trees. There is a white masonry chapel near the center of the cemetery and branching out from it on either side are two semicircular buildings, quite like those at Normandy, with tablets of the missing.

In some ways, the existence of battlefield cemeteries and memorials is odd. Sentiment aside, it might have been more practical and efficient simply to inter the dead in a mass and unmarked grave. Surely, this has been the case in some instances. Certainly, some of the dead of other wars have been so treated, and there are bodies that have been burned or consigned to the sea. However, it is a mark of American culture that the dead have not been forgotten or ignored. Instead, they have been interred in well-marked graves, arranged in symmetrical patterns, and surrounded by the visual beauties of a cultivated space. Their honor is as much a part of the site as is their interment. Similarly, honor has motivated the building of single monuments as well. As noted earlier, ABMC maintains multiple such monuments around the world.

Monuments

Three of the memorial monuments in Washington, DC, were built by the ABMC but are now administered by the US National Park Service. These are the American Expeditionary Forces Memorial commemorating the some 2 million American service personnel who formed the AEF in World War I. This memorial features an 8 foot high bronze statue of General John J. Pershing, who led the AEF. The other two monuments are much better known. They are the World War II Memorial and the Korean

Fig. 6-6 World War II Memorial

War Memorial, both of which have been examined as examples of visual persuasion elsewhere by the author (Ragsdale 2011).

The US National World War II Memorial is located at the end of the Reflecting Pool opposite the Lincoln Memorial. It is a semicircular ring of granite tablets around an oval pond and fountain, which are inscribed with the name of one of the 48 states of the Union at the time of the war as well as other US territories like the US Virgin Islands. The rings of tablets each has as its centerpiece an arched tower, one of which is identified as "Atlantic" and the other as "Pacific." Each tower is ornamented with sculpture. Around the pond at the base of the tablets are smaller tablets depicting scenes from the battles of the war. The monument is stark white.

The Korean War Veterans Memorial is a collection of 19 stainless steel statues of a squad of soldiers spread out in a triangle in full battle dress. Around this tableau are an Honor Roll, a Pool of Remembrance, and a polished black granite Mural Wall, similar to the Vietnam Wall, with 2,400 etched images based on 15,000 Korean War photographs of those who participated in the war. The tableau of soldiers is situated in a sloping field, which is almost park like in nature and which accentuates the visual power of the statues. The stainless steel of the statues glows in daylight.

As with the battlefield cemeteries and memorials, the ABMC is responsible for a large number of individual monuments to World War I battles in Europe. Additionally, there are several such monuments

Fig. 6-7 Korean War Veterans Memorial

commemorating World War II battles in Europe as well as in the Pacific. These monuments have several features in common. First, they are at or near the actual battles they commemorate. Second, and especially important for the purposes of this book, the monuments are set in small parks, which afford the visitor the opportunity to reflect on those events which the monuments represent. Third, the monuments are often extravagant examples of architecture and sculpture, as if to honor the people and events they commemorate with the most compelling structures. There will be six World War I monuments discussed here, the first of which is the Chateau-Thierry American Monument in France.

The Chateau-Thierry monument is two miles west of the village of Chateau-Thierry, and about 54 miles east of Paris. "The monument consists of an impressive double colonnade rising above a long terrace. On its west façade are heroic sculptured figures representing the United States and France. On its east façade is a map showing American military operations in this region and an orientation table pointing out the significant battle sites" (http://www.abmc.gov). The monument is set on a hill surrounded by open lawn and trees overlooking the valley of the Marne River.

Among the best known battles of World War I was fought near the Belgian village of Ypres (now Ieper), called "Wipers" by some of the many British and American troops who fought and died there. One of the battles fought at Ypres, in which the German forces used chlorine gas against the Allied forces, was immortalized in Canadian Lieutenant Colonel John McCrae's poem "In Flanders Field." The Kemmel American Monument commemorating the battles fought here is six miles south of Ypres on the Mont Kemmel Road and overlooks the former battlefield. "This small monument on a low platform consists of a rectangular white stone block, in front of which is carved a soldier's helmet upon a wreath" (http://www.abmc.gov). Behind the monument is a stand of trees.

The Montfaucon American Monument is 20 miles northwest of Verdun in France near the Meuse-Argonne American Cemetery and Memorial. It is a fluted granite Doric column standing on a broad base and rising 200 feet into the air. At the top is a statue symbolizing liberty. The monument is set amidst a stand of trees. The Montsec American Monument commemorates the American forces who fought in the St. Mihiel, France, salient in 1917 and 1918, and is 10 miles east of the town of St. Mihiel. It is an imposing circular colonnade, reminiscent of the Jefferson Memorial in Washington, DC, with a broad stairway up to the open central area where there is a bronze map of the St. Mihiel salient. Finally, the Sommepy Monument, near Reims in northeast France "is essentially a tower of golden-yellow limestone." It sits on a rectangular base on an open lawn surrounded by a dense growth of trees. The Tours American Monument, which lies 146 miles southwest of Paris, differs from the other World War I monuments discussed here in that it honors the work of those who served in the supply service of the American Expeditionary Forces. It sits in a small paved park and "consists of a handsome fountain of white stone with a gold gilded statue of an American Indian holding an eagle" (http://www.abmc.gov).

There are also six World War II ABMC monuments to be considered here. Two of these are to be found in Normandy, France, near the D-Day landing beaches, two are located in the continental United States, and two may be found in the area of the Pacific theatre of World War II. The Utah Beach American Memorial is located "approximately a mile and a half northeast of Sainte-Marie-du-Mont (Manche), France. This monument commemorates the achievements of the American Forces of the VII Corps who landed and fought in the liberation of the Cotentin Peninsula from June 6, 1944 to July 1, 1944. The memorial consists of a red granite obelisk surrounded by a small developed park overlooking the historic sand dunes of Utah Beach, one of the two American landing beaches during the Normandy invasion of June 6, 1944" (http://www.abmc.gov).

Very near the Utah Beach Memorial is the Pointe du Hoc Ranger Monument. The monument is "a simple granite pylon positioned atop a German concrete bunker with tablets at its base inscribed in French and

English." Built by the French, this monument commemorates the assault on a 100 foot cliff by forces of the American Second Ranger Battalion commanded by Lieutenant Colonel James Earl Rudder, who captured the German artillery that might have been directed at the landing forces on Omaha and Utah beaches (http://www.abmc.gov). Lieutenant Colonel Rudder returned to the US a hero and later served notably as the President of Texas A&M University.

On either coast of the continental United States, memorials commemorate service men and women of World War II. The East Coast Memorial is located in New York City's Battery Park at the southern tip of Manhattan. It is a large bronze eagle with spread wings, which "commemorates those soldiers, sailors, marines, coast guardsmen, merchant marines and airmen who met their deaths in the service of their country in the western waters of the Atlantic Ocean. . . . Its axis is oriented on the Statue of Liberty. On each side of the axis are four gray granite pylons upon which are inscribed the name, rank, organization and state of each of the 4,609 missing in the waters of the Atlantic" (http://www.abmc.gov).

In the Presidio in San Francisco, California, is the West Coast Memorial "erected in the memory of those soldiers, sailors, marines, coast guardsmen, and airmen who met their deaths in the American coastal waters of the Pacific Ocean during World War II. It consists of a curved gray granite wall decorated with bas relief sculpture and a statue of liberty on its right flank" (http://www.abmc.gov). The wall has inscribed on it the 412 names, with rank, organization, and state, of those missing in action. Behind the memorial is a grove of trees and nearby is the Golden Gate Bridge.

The final two monuments to be described here are the Honolulu Memorial and the Guadalcanal American Memorial, both of course on Pacific islands. The Honolulu Memorial stands at the entrance to the National Memorial Cemetery of the Pacific located in an extinct volcanic crater known commonly as the Punchbowl. The monument consists of a flight of stairs flanked on either side by five stone walls on which are carved the names of the missing from World War II, the Korean War, and more recently the Vietnam War. At the top of the stairs is a Court of Honor, which contains a chapel and two map galleries. In the front and center of the Court is a 30 foot figure standing on the prow of a US Navy vessel holding a laurel branch. Both the memorial and the cemetery nearby are planted with abundant greenery, trees, and sprawling lawns (http://www.abmc.gov).

Further west in the Pacific on the site in the Solomon Islands of one of the bloodiest battles of World War II is the Guadalcanal American

Memorial. It sits unadorned by trees on a hillside overlooking the town of Honiara. Within its nearly square walled area is a 24 foot tall pylon with four smaller walls arranged so as to point to the major areas of battle. These walls describe the battles and list the lost US naval vessels. Unlike the previous monuments described here, the Guadalcanal American Memorial is quite stark and forbidding (http://www.abmc.gov).

Fig. 6-8 Garden of Remembrance Dublin

America is, of course, not alone in erecting monumental structures to commemorate its service men and women lost in battle. In Liverpool, England, for example, there is St. John's Gardens, a beautifully landscaped and colorful small park with numerous monuments dedicated to regiments in a variety of wars. In Dublin, Ireland, directly across the Irish Sea from Liverpool, there are several war memorial gardens, one of which is a dramatic small park called the Garden of Remembrance. The garden features a sunken reflecting pool shaped in the form of a cross and commemorates all those who fought to obtain Ireland's freedom. Within the park are abundant floral plantings. Finally, there is in the Tiergarten in Berlin a memorial to the Soviet dead from World War II featuring a statue of a soldier in the center of a stoa and containing artillery pieces and tanks from the battle against the Nazis in Berlin.

Hallowed ground, as has been seen, commemorates great battles or battle sites of particular significance so that the living may not forget the events of war. It provides honorable resting places for those who lost their lives in battle. Hallowed ground, perhaps curiously, is also for the living. Much like the pleasure gardens of royalty, the city parks of the world, and national parks, it gives the living a place to rest, to remember, and to relax from the demands of daily life. In each case, human beings turn to the environs of nature, albeit augmented by visual design, to meet these needs.

CHAPTER SEVEN

URBAN DESIGN IN THE ANCIENT CITY

J. DONALD RAGSDALE
AND FRANCES E. BRANDAU-BROWN

Including cities in a book focused on designed spaces would seem at first glance to be a mistake. After all, cities, unlike gardens and parks, are by and large not developed with a single controlling design. They evolve over many years under the control of many designers with often divergent purposes, and most cities show evidence of a strong strain of haphazard development. "Everywhere cities, towns, and suburbs find it difficult to secure coherent and satisfying patterns of development. . . . There is no sum of parts adding up to a greater whole. Strong organizing patterns are missing. . . . The net effect at its worst is of a fractured disjointed world of divisions without connecting seams, a world offering residents no identifiable center other than the buildings in which they live" (Hedman and Jaszewski 1984, 1-2). Yet, within these remarks about cities in general is the implicit desire for "strong organizing patterns," "connecting seams," and "identifiable centers," suggesting that residence in and movement in and around a city call for a unifying set of design principles that facilitate the use of space for living as much as it does in gardens and parks.

Indeed, the Center for Design Excellence (www.urbandesign.org) identifies many of the same elements for urban design that have been noted in Chapter One of this book. They include:

- order
- unity
- balance
- proportion
- scale
- hierarchy
- symmetry
- rhythm
- contrast
- context
- detail

- texture
- harmony
- beauty

Despite the somewhat disparaging tone of the first paragraph of this chapter, it turns out that cities, like other spaces, can be assessed as visual persuasion according to their elements. Compelling form in the city is, of course, a complicated business. The comparative age of the city's buildings, for example, usually results in such differences of architectural style that maintaining a sense of unity or of visual harmony is quite challenging, especially if principles of urban design are ignored. In assessing cities, with their inevitable multiple, adjacent buildings, it is also true that unique considerations are present. It is not just the buildings themselves in relation to one another, but it is also the design of the space between them or context that must be considered. Additionally, when considering buildings, as opposed to a single building, there is the obvious consideration of rhythm.

Hedman and Jaszewski (1984) deal with some of the complications of assessing the visual persuasiveness of a city as opposed to a building or a park or a garden in their analysis of the row of Queen Anne houses in San Francisco, CA, known popularly as the Painted Ladies. "This particular group of row houses combines a powerful sense of unity with considerable design variation" (15). The authors take particular note of the similar pitch and scale of the roofs, the notches between each street façade, similarly proportioned windows, and common types of entryways among other elements. This assessment, from the standpoint of visual persuasion, is not so different from the assessment of a single building as much as it is more complex.

Were cities developed from the beginning according to urban design principles, some elements of their design should be evident by merely looking at a map. The layout of streets, bridges, and buildings would have a noticeable aesthetic appeal. This is so in many cases. An overhead view of Paris, for example, and perhaps Berlin, reveals in particular how streets leading into and out of the city's center evoke aesthetic responses. The tree-lined Champs Élysées in Paris and the Strasse des 17 juni passing through the Tiergarten in Berlin and connecting to Unter den Linden are especially noteworthy in this regard. However, there is much more to the visual persuasiveness of a city than just its aesthetic appeal. Monuments, churches and cathedrals, government buildings, and public squares are not situated just anywhere but are placed according to notions of where such structures ought to be placed. Certainly, the ancient Greeks thought this way as we shall see.

In dealing with the visual influence of cities in this and the following chapter, therefore, a combination of the elemental and the semiotic approaches will be necessary fully to assess the impact of urban design. Some aspects of urban design, as noted, have to do almost exclusively with the visual experience of the resident or visitor. As in a visit to a garden or park, the question has to do with the feelings one has within the city. Is the city aesthetically pleasing? Other aspects have to do with the symbolic value of location or site, and answer such questions as what is the significance of placing a temple on the highest point in a city or locating the city center on the banks of a river or at the convergence of several avenues. Chapters One and Two have established those elements of visual design which may be used to assess the experience of being in a city. For ideas about the semiotic principles which enter into urban design, it is useful to begin with an examination of ancient Greece and especially Athens.

For this inquiry it is insightful to take note of the subtitle of Wycherly's (1976) book *How the Greeks Built Cities: The relationship of architecture and town planning to everyday life in ancient Greece*. While appearance of the city was of concern to the Greeks, the facilitation of everyday life was the preeminent goal. Visual influence, therefore, was intended primarily to make daily life harmonious and pleasant. A citizen was supposed to feel comfortable, among other things, as he or she went from place to place during the day. As this examination proceeds, a number of principles of Greek town planning will be identified and, along with the use of visual design principles, the city of Athens will be assessed as visual persuasion. Then, the chapter will turn its focus to the ancient city of Rome to see whether or not the elemental features of the city and the semiotic values carry forward those of ancient Athens. Finally, ancient Paris will be examined in the same way, seeking in each case to answer the question of whether or not cities may be seen as visually influential. It is indeed fortunate that there is a guide available written by the Roman architect Vitruvius, whose *Ten Books on Architecture* (1960) were based on his thorough knowledge of Greek buildings and cities.

It is worth noting at this juncture that for Vitruvius the practice of architecture—and for Vitruvius this included the design and building of cities—was reducible to three simple goals: *utilitas, firmitas,* and *venustas.* Buildings and cities should fulfill the function for which they were built, should be strong in construction, and should be beautiful. It is important to examine Vitruvius's concept of beauty as it relates to visual persuasion.

Unfortunately, Vitruvius does not spend much time in explaining himself. In speaking in general of the basic principles of architecture, Vitruvius lists order, arrangement, eurythmy, symmetry, propriety, and economy. As with many ancient texts, these terms are not so clear today as they undoubtedly were in Rome. Order, for example, appears to arise when the parts or modules of a building are all in harmony with each other and when they are symmetrical and in proper proportion to one another. The idea of thinking of a building as a set of modules rather than as an organic whole seems quaint today, but it is not an irrelevant way of thinking.

Arrangement proceeds directly from order and has to do with "the putting of things in their proper places" (Vitruvius 1960, 13). "Eurythmy is beauty and fitness in the adjustments of the members" (14). This beauty and fitness come about when a building's dimensions are properly proportioned. Eurythmy also requires symmetry, which Vitruvius includes as a separate principle. Appropriateness was an important consideration in many of the Classical arts, such as oratory, and architecture is no exception. The Greeks, and later the Romans, thought of art as arising from adherence to a set of rules. The Greek word was *techne.* Vitruvius explains that propriety comes from "prescription . . . usage . . . or from nature." One particularly helpful example he gives is that a building with an elegant interior also ought to have an elegant entrance. Economy, finally, has to do with costs and the use of materials. There is no statement about precisely which design elements would generate either a beautiful building or a beautiful city. Beauty is the result of a pleasing appearance in good taste "and when its members are in due proportion according to correct principles of symmetry" (17).

The design of cities, for Vitruvius, had a great deal to do with finding a site or location where the wind and weather in general could be either controlled or accommodated and where there would be both an ample water supply and fertile soil. The first consideration, for example, in the location of a town was "a very healthy site" (Vitruvius 1960, 17). Streets were to be laid out to minimize the effects of both hot and cold winds. Vitruvius suggests where temples to various gods should be placed without specifying reasons in any specific sense. Similarly, locations for the forum, basilicas, and theatres all are indicated, but it is clear that Vitruvius was much less concerned in the ten books with explaining general principles than in offering prescriptions. However, it is evident from more contemporary research into city building in ancient Greece just what some of those principles probably were.

In saying that strength, functionality, and beauty were the fundamental principles of architecture, Vitruvius was simply carrying forward the Greek

Fig. 7-1 Athenian Acropolis and Parthenon

sensibility that beauty was fundamental to all of life. "Architects, like all Greek artists, unerringly seized upon the opportunity offered for the creation of new beauty" (Wycherley 1976, 29). The Greeks simply saw aesthetic appeal as a universal goal. Unfortunately, one must guess at just what the means of achieving the goal were in the design of cities. Even Vitruvius does not lay down a set of guidelines. However, an examination of ancient Greek city building does reveal a number of characteristics which would suggest what the sources of visual influence were. This examination focuses on the acropolis, the agora, types of buildings, the layout of city streets, and the question to be answered is how these aspects contributed to the visual impact of the city.

The acropolis of a Greek city was a hill, presumably the city's highest point, which could easily be defended from intruders. Greek cities were walled, but walls came well after the city itself was built. The acropolis would provide a place of refuge and defense even at the beginning of the city as well as after the outer fortifications were completed. Naturally, an acropolis, and the astute reader will surely have in mind the Athenian one, drew the eye upward toward the sky. "One should remember that there is *no* clear line between religious and secular in Greek architecture, any more than in Greek life. . . . The relation could be expressed in various ways; the god watched over the city; the city belonged to the god, in a sense it was his shrine, and dedicated to him. The acropolis had its special sanctity, and so had the agora" (Wycherley 1976, 87). Since "the temple represents the flower of Greek architecture," it is not surprising to find the most important temples located on the acropolis. In Athens, for example, the Parthenon, the temple of Athena who was the god of the city, is the largest temple on the acropolis. Several less important temples are located there as well, including the Erechtheion and the Temple of Athena Nike. It is not hard to imagine the view of the Athenian acropolis by someone standing below it, so it is the design elements of location and vertical line which dominate the city's skyline. Both of these elements are in accord with Greek religious views. Of course, it is not merely the hill itself which is visually influential but the integration of the site with the beauty of that which is built there.

It is impossible to ignore the overall significance of the Athenian acropolis, especially for a work such as this one on visual persuasion. "The creation of the Athenian Acropolis required, to some degree, the invention of the art of architecture itself. For example, when we study the system of proportions by which a classical Greek temple was composed, we are witnessing the birth of the idea that the human mind and eye are affected by the mathematical balance of aesthetic elements in a visual composition. We behold . . . the invention of the very concept that there is such a thing as proportional balance" (Tung 2003, 249-250). Here we see the origins of the ideas of compelling form, suggesting the immediate and powerful visual impact of a structure.

The Greek city radiated out and down from the acropolis, either in a circle or more often on one side of the hill. The heart of that part of the city was the agora. As Wycherley says (1976, 50), the term "agora" is not readily translatable into English because of its unique Hellenic character. City center does not do it justice, neither does town square. "It was the constant resort of all citizens, and it did not spring to life on special occasions but was the daily scene of social life, business and politics." Civic center, given its modern usage, may come closest to capturing the idea of the agora. The area was a flat, expansive surface surrounded by temples and stoa, or roofed colonnades, places where orators could speak to the crowds and where trial by jury could occur, shops, government buildings, and similar structures. Some agoras had the shape of theatres, although actual theatres were set away from the agora.

What was the visual significance of the agora? It was the sign of and the place for the practice of democracy. Here is where public debates were held, where trials took place, where the gods were honored, where produce and meat could be purchased, and where citizens could meet for discussions both serious and casual. "At various moments in the history of Athens, a visitor might find Socrates teaching philosophy . . . witness a law court in session . . . hear a political debate of one of the city's official assemblies . . . [or] observe a religious ceremony" (Tung 2003, 254). The agora not only signified the democratic nature of Greek society at the time, its location at the rough geographic center of the city reinforced the centrality of the activities that took place there. It was the heart of the city, from which all else radiated and to which all would come on a given day. Statues and temples reminded the visitor to the agora of the beauty of daily life. Cities like Athens had, in addition to an acropolis and an agora, numerous other public and official places, such as a gymnasium, a stadium, and a theatre. All of these structures roughly formed the main part of the city proper, while personal residences were located away from the center.

Greek cities commonly used a gridiron or chessboard layout of streets, wherein streets crossed each other at right angles and where city blocks provided space for the building of personal residences. This gridiron or chessboard pattern is particularly evident at Miletus and Olynthus (Wycherley 1976). Certainly, the layout of streets had to conform to the geography of the city. Hills especially had to be accommodated, but the regularity and symmetry of the gridiron or chessboard plan must have appealed to the Greeks' sense of appropriateness and what Vitruvius called eurythmy. The Greek city was a space designed to give ease to daily life by putting those activities necessary for survival close together. At every juncture, especially on the acropolis and in the agora, the Greek citizen was visually aware of the architectural splendor of the memorial statues and the temples. He or she could look upward to the largest temples on the acropolis and be reminded that religious belief permeated the Greek city, and, of course, the acropolis drew the eyes to the heavens. Then the citizen of a Greek city could follow a simple and regular and aesthetically pleasing pattern of streets to his or her personal residence. Visual influence was a primary factor in the planning of a Greek city.

Athenian urban planning was unfortunately not entirely successful in its visual and perhaps idealistic intent. Ancient Athens was the result of "one of civilization's most remarkable outbursts of intellectual invention" (Tung 2003, 250). However, "on the slopes below the Acropolis, even at the moment of its creation, [it] was a remarkably ugly, disorganized, and unsanitary city." Before turning attention to the visual significance of Ancient Rome, it should also be acknowledged that this city too was in many places unclean, disorderly, overcrowded, and unsanitary. While examining the visual power of any city, it would be hard, perhaps impossible, to find one that did not also have its grimy and unkempt side. Approaching Paris, for example, from Aéroport Charles de Gaulle via the *banlieue* on the city's north side for the first time, one would hardly guess this to be the "City of Light."

It is well-known the extent to which ancient Rome was influenced by ancient and Hellenistic Greece. Modern museums are filled with Roman imitations of Greek sculpture and other art. However, city planning in ancient Rome did not imitate that in Greece, and the visual power of the Colosseum, the Forum, Trajan's Forum, the Capitoline Hill, and other striking aspects reveal a rather different set of semiotic and visually elemental features at work.

Today's visitor to Rome cannot, of course, do anything more than imagine how the ancient city looked. Thanks to years during which the city's buildings were ransacked for their marble and limestone for use on other structures and ravaged by plundering invaders, there is little left to aid in visualization. Standing on the Palatine Hill above the ruins of the Roman forum, what one sees is hardly more than that of a rubble pile. Even through reconstructions of the city at its apex of development, the layout of the Forum, Hadrian's Forum, and the Colosseum suggest a crowded cluster of buildings with no aesthetic principles at all guiding their placement. How, then, could one consider ancient Rome to be visually compelling?

The answer to this question emerges from a consideration of the semiotics of the city. Just as the acropolis and the agora had symbolic value for Athenians because of their placement and the structures erected on and in them, so too does Rome's city core (Tung 2003). Under the reign of Augustus (27 BCE—14 CE) Rome underwent a building campaign that transformed the city. This building campaign was intended to demonstrate the strength and dominance of the Roman Empire. The buildings and their placement were designed to be a persuasive message for both the citizens and the enemies of Rome. Augustus wanted to be remembered as the architect of the Republic. His goal was to "create symbols that effectively could convey his legacy in a preserved state, impervious to the wear of time" (Lauer 2004, 426). Augustus understood that the buildings could be used to shape and create a public narrative and store a collective memory. A remark famously attributed to Augustus is that he transformed Rome from a city of brick into a city of marble. This remark refers both to the actual physical transformation of the city under his building program and to the metaphorical transformation of the Republic into an ancient super power.

Fig. 7-2 Roman Forum

Walking through the streets of ancient Rome was to be immersed in the visual rhetoric of its leaders. Lamp (2011) maintained that although not all of the citizens were educated in rhetorical argument, through cultural literacy and involvement they came to be aware of the meaning and iconicity of the buildings and their ornamentation. Roman orators often used the strategy of location to aid memory, so the buildings in the environment where speeches were delivered helped the orator remember the content of his message. Using the buildings and their architectural features created an interplay between the structure and the message. The buildings were adorned with *bas reliefs* and statuary to celebrate leaders, victories, and gods, and these helped the speaker remember the content of his speech. By referencing these features in the speech, the items took on the meaning of the orator's argument. Augustus established a speaking forum on the Palatine and imbued the "entire site with new visual cues suggesting the emperor's spiritual connections to the Republic and his divine associations" (Lauer 2004, 434). This attempt to establish a connection between the government, its leaders, and the divine is similar to that seen in ancient Greece.

Rome was said to be a city of 250,000 men. Add to that slaves, women, and children, and the city probably had 1 million inhabitants. "No other city in Europe would attain this size until London did so in the 1820s during the Industrial Revolution" (Tung 2003, 31). The most wealthy and powerful citizens lived on Palatine Hill with a view of the bustling activity in the Forum below. Overlooking the richly decorated government buildings and temples, the inhabitants surely felt the power of the Republic and the omnipresence of the Gods. In addition, the size, scale, and expense of these buildings sent a message of what it meant to be a member of the powerful ruling class, and they served as a warning for those who might cross the Empire.

The significance of the structures was reinforced by Rome's restrictive building program, meaning that there were only limited occasions for erecting public buildings and monuments. According to Lamp (2011), building monuments was a right reserved for triumphant generals or magistrates, and Senate approval was required. Building projects had to have consensus and the sponsor had to have some degree of popularity. This was so because the building was basically a state-sanctioned endorsement of that individual.

One example of a building constructed to honor a specific event is the Temple of Mars. It was designed to celebrate Augustus' victory at the battle of Philippi. "The temple of Mars was linked to the memory of Augustus's battle at Philippi, both by the event it was meant to commemorate, as well as its use" (Lamp 2011, 185). The Temple was decorated with tapestries and statues, most notably a statue of Augustus in full military dress. All around the Temple there were inscriptions proclaiming his victory and his place in Roman history. The Senate met in the Temple to discuss war and military victories, so it was used as both a reminder of historical victories and as the place to stage future wins. The Temple is thus a good example of the importance of visual imagery in Roman culture.

The Temple of Mars is just one example of structures that can be found in the Forum. The Forum is bordered by Capitoline Hill, Velian Hill, the Basilica Aemilia and the Basilica Julia. The Forum grew up organically over centuries with buildings and monuments being added by new politicians so that the finite space became cluttered. Just outside the heart of the Forum sits the Roman Colosseum. Its construction began under Vespasian in 72 CE and was completed under Titus in 80 CE. The Colosseum provided entertainment for the citizens and also reinforced

Fig. 7-3 Colosseum

social rank. For example, those with the most power and influence had the best seats to watch the gladiators do battle and to watch the slaughter of thousands of animals. Rome's festivals and military victories were celebrated in both the Forum and Colosseum. The Colosseum is an iconic structure which had significant meaning to the citizens. An inscription on the site says that the emperor Vespasian ordered the new amphitheater to be erected from his general's share of war booty. The structure was seen as a triumphant moment for Rome and as a place for celebrating great victories. In addition to the inscription, the amphitheater had a beautiful and rhythmic pattern of arches decorated with bronze shields and filled with painted statues of gods or emperors. All of these contributed to the iconicity and visual power of the Colosseum.

In addition to the buildings in the Forum and the Colosseum, military victories were celebrated with huge arches decorated with scenes from triumphant battles. The reliefs on the arches told the story of victories and served as a part of the cultural narrative that reinforced the strength of the Roman army. Two famous arches were the Arch of Constantine and the Arch of Titus. Each commemorated its namesake's victory and would provide the route taken by Roman emperors when they returned to the city after a battle. For example, Constantine's route lead through the Circus Maximus, around Palatine Hill, then along the Sacra to the Forum, passing the Arch of Titus and the Arch of Septimius Severus.

Clearly these arches are icons, because they are decorated with images of the victories and they are a part of the celebration. Rome's arches, buildings, and monuments all create a cityscape of meaning. The visually persuasive power of the city structures was not lost on any of the Roman leaders. Augustus was the first to set about leaving his legacy in stone. The greatest of the Roman orators, Cicero, also knew the persuasive power of location and structure. He was said to have purchased property that would keep him in view of Rome's citizens. Vasaly (1993) said that Cicero was known to use gestures toward buildings imbued with meaning. Clearly, these adornments and buildings were iconic because they had meaning for the constituency. Vasaly noted that Cicero realized that "great oratory, like great drama, demands both an audience and a stage" (40). The significance of the location and the structures contained in that location were key elements in Cicero's oratorical power.

Ancient Rome was full of iconic structures that were intentionally placed and decorated to demonstrate the power of Rome to its citizens and all who visited. According to Lamp (2011), Roman orators routinely used the memory evoked by a place or object in their rhetoric. Second, the same structure could then take on the new meaning and emotion created by the orator in his speech. Third, Roman citizens' "familiarity with the mnemonic [memory] system predisposed them to look for visual narratives in the environment" (188). Finally, the Augustan building campaign led to the creation of a visually compelling cityscape. Lamp concluded that the buildings, monuments, statues, and arches all served to instruct audiences about how they should conceptualize and participate in the new Roman Empire. Visual messages were everywhere for the Roman inhabitants.

Today's Paris is one of the most visually impressive and, indeed, beautiful cities in the world, but early Paris gave only a glimpse of the city it was to become. Initially, Paris was an Iron Age settlement on the Île de la Cité in the middle of the River Seine, and the home of a tribe of Celtic or Gaulish people known as the Parisii. The settlement was located in a fertile plain along a well-traveled north-south axis which was used for trading tin (Jones 2005). Recent excavations in nearby Bercy suggest that the primary location of the settlement may not have been on the island but rather on the right bank of the Seine in what is today the 12th arrondissement, or administrative section, of the city. By the time of the Roman conquest of most of present-day France, however, the principal settlement was indeed on the island.

The Parisii appear to have understood well the importance of location for the purposes of commerce and defense. The Seine afforded commerce and also made the island an easy location to defend. Although it may not necessarily have been a factor in the view of the Parisii, the settlement's location on an island in a river heightened its visual significance from the standpoint of visitors, or enemies, approaching from the north or the south. The location stood out visually much in the same way as did the Athenian Acropolis. It stood out to the viewer as a result of its water border, making isolation rather than height its principal visual feature. Although today there is only one other island nearby, the Île St. Louis, there were originally three islands upstream from the Île de la Cité. The settlement itself, then, would have been what caught the eye of the visitor.

Fig. 7-4 Musée de Cluny Interior

During the expansion of the Roman Republic in the 1st century BCE, Julius Caesar conquered the Parisii and placed their territory under Roman rule. Caesar called the settlement of the Parisii Lutetia. Caesar's lieutenant, Labenius, defeated the Gallic leader, Camulogenus, in Grenelle or Auteuil to the west. Those Parisii who survived joined forces in the south with Vercingétorix, whose band was defeated at the battle of Alesia in 52 BCE (Jones 2005, 7). At this historical juncture, Lutetia fell under the influence of its Roman conquerors who now settled there.

The city's urban development took some time, although a gridiron pattern of streets appears to have been laid out quite quickly. A basilica was eventually constructed on the Île, but it was not completed until the 4th century CE. A cathedral dedicated to Saint-Étienne was erected. While little is known about this structure, it is notable that it was built in the same location as the 12th century cathedral of Notre-Dame (Jones 2005). From a visually influential perspective, the Île now not only called attention to itself by its location within the Seine, it exhibited the trappings of governmental and ecclesiastical power.

The Romans expanded their development of Lutetia onto the land to the south of the original settlement. Much of Roman Lutetia was located on the left bank of the Seine in what is today the 5th arrondissement. There, settlers soon built several characteristically Roman structures for the new inhabitants: an amphitheatre or arena, a theatre, a temple/basilica, three baths, and an aqueduct to supply potable water. Two of these structures remain today: the Arènes de Lutèce and the public bath complex on the present-day Boulevard Saint-Germain. These baths form part of the Musée de Cluny. Visually, these Roman structures gave Lutetia some of the air of Rome itself. Though not on the scale of Rome, Lutetia would have appeared to its citizens and its visitors as a quite harmonious and pleasant city, complete with most of the trappings of what at the time constituted advanced civilization. It had a typical Roman order and beauty, such that the Roman Emperor Julian, who stayed there in 358 CE and again in 360-361 CE, was moved to call the city that would shortly be named Paris his "beloved Lutetia" (Jones 2005, 1).

If ancient Athens, Imperial Rome, and early Paris are indicative, and it seems clear that they are, then cities are like other designed spaces in their compelling visual power. In these ancient cities, it is possible to see many elements of design as well as a number of icons and indexes. Unfortunately, development on the fringes could not match that of the cities' centers, and slums and filth could readily be found in both Athens and Rome. What the ancient cities evidence above all, however, is the thoroughgoing effort by designers and builders to influence the thoughts and the feelings of both city dwellers and visitors. If anything, urban design in the cities to be examined in the following chapter demonstrates this effort to an even greater degree.

CHAPTER EIGHT

URBAN DESIGN IN THE MODERN CITY

Cities as spaces have dual goals. First, as noted, cities are designed to influence the thoughts and feelings of both residents and visitors. Cities seem to be designed in large measure to address the following questions among others. Is there sufficient space for housing and for meeting the needs of residents for food and drink, entertainment, work, and safety? Is the layout of the city conducive to easy access to essential services? Is there sufficient public transportation? Is there open space to relieve the congestion of the city's structures? Are there sufficient green spaces—parks and gardens—to provide rest, recuperation, and reflection?

Second, cities seem to have the goal of establishing status and prestige as well as power in comparison to other cities both in the same country and abroad. City design, therefore, addresses another set of questions. Does the skyline of the city convey strength or power? Are there iconic structures—commercial buildings, governmental and educational structures, monuments, memorials, museums, libraries—to suggest the prestige of the city? Is the architecture eclectic or homogeneous? Whichever the case, is it visually compelling? Is the city colorful—steel, glass, painted surfaces, slate, metals of other kinds? Is there water to suggest life and to aid in cooling the atmosphere? In this chapter, a wide variety of visually impressive cities will be examined with a view toward exemplifying these dual persuasive purposes.

Most of the museums discussed in this chapter are more completely addressed in their role of means of visual persuasion in previous works by the author (Ragsdale 2009a, 2009b) and will not be assessed in detail here. Additionally, skyscrapers, governmental buildings, churches and cathedrals, university buildings, and other city structures are assessed in more detail in another volume (Ragsdale 2011). Then, there are numerous occasions in this chapter where parks and gardens are mentioned whose fuller discussion may be found elsewhere in this book.

Paris, the City of Light, is for many the epitome of visual impressiveness in a city. There are several reasons for this, each of which could be thought of as an essential element of good urban design. First, Paris is an eminently livable city. There is an abundance of residential real estate throughout the 20 administrative divisions, or *arrondissements*, of the city. Additionally, there are grocery stores, outdoor markets, bakeries,

Fig. 8-1 Champs Élysées

pharmacies, bistros, and the other similar agencies necessary to sustain daily life scattered throughout the city and within easy walking distance of the apartments and homes of Parisian citizens. Workplaces are similarly accessible. The Paris Metro, one of the most extensive sets of lines in the world, is equally accessible, making any location within or on the periphery of the city a short ride away. For those times of rest and relaxation, Paris's many parks are sprinkled throughout the metropolitan area. There are two major airports and several railway stations, which facilitate travel outside the city. Charles de Gaulle Airport is in the suburb of Roissy-en-France north of Paris, and Orly Airport is in the southern suburbs of Orly and Villeneuve-le-Roi. The railway stations are within the city limits and connected to the Metro lines. These things which make Paris livable also make it a very easy city to visit as a tourist.

In addition to its livability, Paris is also a compelling visual experience. Although there are many architectural styles within the city, the preponderance of the French Baroque style, as seen in the Louvre, makes for a consistent, homogeneous, and graceful set of visual images. The city of Paris has been careful to confine its modern skyscrapers primarily to the western suburb of Puteaux in the area known as La Défense. Even in that area, however, the architecture is homogeneous. Many of the city's streets are also visually compelling. The best known of these streets, the Champs Élysées, offers a broad vista with trees along each side as it extends from the Arc de Triomphe to the Tuileries Gardens. Indeed, Paris is an axial city in that this street connects La Défense in the west to the Tuileries and the Louvre in the east. On a clear day, the view along a horizontal line from west to east or vice versa is visually dramatic with La Grand Arche de la Défense, the Arc de Triomphe, and the Luxor obelisk in the Place de la Concorde all in view.

Throughout the city, there are structures which are not only visually compelling but also iconic. The list reads like a set of tourist destinations, which indeed it is. There are the museums—the Louvre, the Musée d'Orsay, the Musée Picasso, and the Centre Georges Pompidou to name only the most prominent ones. Museums have several purposes, among them to preserve paintings and other art objects, to educate visitors, to persuade, and the like. The persuasive function (Ragsdale 2008b) includes serving as an icon for the city of Paris. This is accomplished in three ways: by collecting an impressive array of art, by displaying the art in a dramatic way designed to make it visually compelling, and by housing the collection in a magnificent architectural structure.

The Louvre has without question the world's most extensive and impressive collection, and it is careful to display the collection in the most influential fashion. Nike of Samothrace, for example, is located on a landing at the head of a staircase, and Venus de Milo is situated in the middle of a principle corridor. The building was formerly a palace itself designed and decorated as if it were an object of art. There can be no question that the Louvre gives the city of Paris a prestige that is in accord with the idea of a great city. As a means of visual persuasion, the Louvre is Paris's strongest argument that the city is the center of the universe of art.

Then there are Paris's churches—Notre-Dame, la Sainte-Chapelle, Saint-Sulpice, and le Sacré-Coeur. As with the museums, these four churches are merely the most prominent of a legion of churches in the city. All are excellent specimens of compelling architectural styles, including Gothic and Byzantine. The Opéra Garnier is among the world's most visually compelling performance halls, the Tour Eiffel is a unique symbol of the city, and Les Invalides—the location of the tomb of Napoléon I—is most striking with its gold dome. The reader who is familiar with Paris will note how superficial this list is, since the city is virtually a museum in itself. However, it is equally noticeable that most of the world's great cities cannot compare to Paris even were these structures the only ones to be found there.

Fig. 8-2 Siegessäule at Grosser Stern

As noted in the previous chapter, Paris is located on either side of the River Seine and on islands in that river's center. The original builders of the city undoubtedly selected their island location with commerce and defense in mind, but rivers—or water sources in general—add considerably to the visual impressiveness of the city. Water is both literally and figuratively a source of life. The flow of the Seine is gentle and bucolic. Like the parks and gardens of Paris, the river is an element of nature at the very heart of the stone and concrete structures of the city. The second city to be examined here is also an axial one, and like Paris its axis is visually dramatic and compelling. That city is Berlin, which, although it is still recovering from the extensive damage to it by Allied bombing during World War II, has been largely restored to its pre-war visual prominence.

The axis which defines Berlin is different from that which defines Paris, but it is no less dramatic. On the western edge of Berlin there begins the Tiergarten and the Zoologischer Garten examined in previous chapters, which extend to the location of the Reichstag and the Brandenburg Gate. Through the Tiergarten, Strasse des 17 juni flows from west to east. Near the center of the heavily wooded Tiergarten, several streets converge on the Strasse des 17 juni at the Grosser Stern, where there is centered in a roundabout the gold encrusted Victory Column or Siegessäule. From any perspective, whether walking, driving, or viewing the Tiergarten and its avenues from above, the visual effects are quite dramatic. In only a few of the world's great cities is it possible to be immersed in a forest only to emerge at the site of such revered and compelling architectural structures as the Reichstag and the Brandenburg Gate. As one passes through the

Fig. 8-3 Unter den Linden

Brandenburg Gate into Pariser Platz, the east-west axis continues via Unter den Linden, the storied former carriage path of the Hohenzollern royalty. Also at Pariser Platz, there is the visually impressive architecture of the United States Embassy, the French Embassy, and the Hotel Adlon, the latter of which was almost completely destroyed by Allied bombing in the war. A little further east is the massive Russian Embassy.

Unter den Linden is a boulevard lined on both sides, like the Champs Élysées in Paris, with shops and restaurants. In the center of the avenue, there is a tree-lined green strip with a footpath, allowing pedestrians a pleasant stroll along the path. Almost a park in itself, it is visually becoming. Further east, and as the boulevard becomes a wide street, there is the famous and architecturally compelling Humboldt University, the Neue Wache, and the German History Museum on the north, and on the south side of the street there is the Opera and more buildings of the university. Proceeding east from here, one crosses onto the island in the River Spree known as Museumsinsel.

There are five quite important museums located close together on Museumsinsel, although they are not of the art historical stature of Paris's museums. Their architecture is visually compelling, nonetheless, with the Altes Museum built in the manner of a Greek temple. Museumsinsel was part of the Soviet sector of Berlin following World War II, and the restoration of the island and its museums was not the priority it has become since the unification of East and West Berlin after the fall of the wall. The collections are such as to attract art historians and tourists from aroung the world.

Fig. 8-4 Sony Center Interior

In the Pergamon Museum, there are the remnants of the Pergamon altar from a Greek temple of about the 2nd century BCE and a restored Ishtar Gate from 6th century BCE Babylon. In the Egyptian Museum of the Neues Museum is the bust of Nefertiti, a feature of virtually every introductory text in art and art history. The Alte Nationalgalerie houses European masters and especially works of German painters. The collections and their display contribute to the iconic status of these museums. Important, iconic museums are essential ingredients of visually compelling cities, therefore Museumsinsel is crucial to the visual power of the city of Berlin. However, museums located elsewhere in Berlin also make an important contribution.

Just west of the newly restored Potsdamer Platz, one finds the Gemäldegalerie, with its collection of traditional European masters, and the Neue Nationalgalerie, designed by Mies van der Rohe, with its collection of modern and contemporary masters. In Potsdamer Platz proper, the centerpiece structure is the Sony Center, which houses the Deutsche Kinemathek Film and TV Museum featuring stills, posters, and equipment from the Golden Age of German film before the rise of Adolf Hitler.

The Sony Center is a commanding visual structure. Its white tent-like exterior houses a number of businesses and is the centerpiece of this reclaimed part of Berlin. In turn, the Sony Center is surrounded by skyscrapers housing other businesses and hotels. Within the Center is an open, circular atrium, which features a bandstand, a multiplex cinema, and a number of cafés and restaurants. Much of Berlin features traditional homogeneous architecture, as one finds in Paris. Though Potsdamer Platz is modern in its architecture, it is nonetheless homogeneous.

Fig. 8-5 Gendarmenmarkt

South of Unter den Linden is a large, open square known as Gendarmenmarkt. On either side of this symmetrical square is a German cathedral and a French one, and there is also the Berlin Symphony concert hall. Both of the cathedrals are large and extravagant examples of Neoclassical architecture. Ringing the square are cafés, restaurants, a hotel, and Fassbender and Rausch, ostensibly the largest chocolate store in

Europe. However, it is the open, symmetrical square with its massive
church architecture that is so visually compelling.

Like Paris, Berlin is eminently livable. Sprinkled throughout both the
eastern and western areas of the city are apartments and houses which
afford their residents easy access to the necessities of daily life as well as
to the city's U-Bahn and S-Bahn lines, which whisk the traveler easily to
most areas of the city. Berlin's many gardens and parks give the city's
residents and visitors an opportunity to find respite from the city itself.
Then, as in Paris, there is a river—the Spree—gently rolling through the
city. The next city to be considered here is also built on either side of an
important river, so much so that the River Thames and London are almost
synonymous.

Fig. 8-6 St. Paul's and Millennium Bridge

Although London is not an axial city in the same sense as Paris and
Berlin, it is centered around the east-west flow of the River Thames, and
much of the city's visual power comes from structures built along the
river. Until recent years, the area of London south of the Thames was
rather run down and seedy, particularly in the east end, but the city has
made a noticeable effort to reclaim this area through commercial and
recreational development. Some of this reclamation is visually impressive

as a result of iconic structures having been erected. Three come immediately to mind. In the far east end, there is the development of the O_2 indoor arena, which has brought a wide variety of concerts and sporting events to the city. Closer to the city center is the new Globe Theatre, a near exact replica of Shakespeare's Globe, and adjacent to the Globe is the Tate Modern. The latter is a surprisingly successful conversion of an electric power generating plant into a museum of modern and contemporary art. Crossing the Thames at this location, is the Millennium Bridge, an angular, modern pedestrian suspension structure. The bridge itself is visually compelling but no less so than the view of the city in either direction. Crossing south to Bankside, one's view is dominated by the Globe and the towering smokestack of the Tate Modern. Crossing north, there is a spectacular view of St. Paul's Cathedral.

Fig. 8-7 Trafalgar Square and Nelson Memorial

For most visitors, and, for that matter, residents, it is the north bank of the Thames that is really the home of dozens of iconic and visually compelling structures. These include the Palace of Westminster and Westminster Abbey along with Big Ben right on the banks of the Thames. Proceeding uphill from these iconic buildings there is No. 10 Downing Street, the home of the British Prime Minister, the Banqueting House, and, on arrival at the hilltop, Trafalgar Square with its lions and Nelson Memorial. Surrounding this popular meeting place and location for outdoor concerts and rallies are numerous restaurants and hotels, as well as the Church of St.

Martin-in-the-Fields. On the north side of the square are the London National Gallery and National Portrait Gallery, among the most prestigious museums in the world.

Elsewhere in the city, there are numerous theatres known the world over for their excellent performances. Indeed, London is regarded by many as the premier live performance venue in the world, and many Americans regard a trip to London without seeing a play as a wasted one. There are also the world class department stores, such as Harrod's, one of the largest department stores in the world, Marks and Spencer, and Selfridge's, as well as the men's tailors of Savile Row.

Fig. 8-8 Tower of London Complex

Other iconic structures include the Tower of London, with the Crown Jewels on display in one of the Tower complex's buildings. Most visitors also find the nearby Tower Bridge to be visually compelling as well. London also has Buckingham Palace, one of the official residences of the Queen, where the ceremony of the changing of the guard draws hundreds of visitors and residents alike. Of course, like Paris, London is a city of museums. The most compelling one of these in terms of its building and its collection is the British Museum, centrally located north and east of Trafalgar Square, but there are also The Tate, downstream on the Thames from the Tate Modern, the Victoria and Albert Museum near Kensington housing the world's largest collection of decorative arts, and the Natural History Museum.

Is London a livable city, as Paris and Berlin are? Its streets are not laid out in any geometrically sensible way, but one would have no problem moving about the city on the Underground, on a double-decker red bus, or in one of the city's trademark black taxis. Shops abound, from the most humble street corner grocery to the posh Fortnum and Mason's. The apartments and homes in London are, for the most part, compelling pieces of architecture in the Palladian style. London's parks, as noted earlier, are extensive and numerous, affording respite from the stress of the city. From any perspective, London is a visually powerful city, from its churches and cathedrals, to its museums and governmental buildings to its sheer livability, to the centrality of the Thames. While Paris, Berlin, and London are perhaps the Big Three Western European cities, there are at least two Eastern European cities whose visual power makes them worth a brief examination. These are Prague, in the Czech Republic, and Poznan, Poland.

Prague was fortunate enough during World War II to have escaped the destructiveness of Allied bombing, and although it was in the zone of Soviet influence following the war it did not suffer from a lack of rebuilding efforts. The visual power of Prague today is thus almost entirely the city's heritage from the past. Like other great cities, Prague sits on either side of a river—the Vltava (Moldau)—a body of water that provides both the beauty and the tranquility of nature in the midst of a bustling city. On the left bank of the Vltava is the Old Town, largely a flat area of the city, but on the right bank is the hill of Hradčany, the location of Prague Castle and the Gothic St. Vitus's Cathedral. Within the castle walls are also several small flower gardens. These structures are not only architecturally compelling, but their presence on the hill gives them an additional visual power. In turn, the view of Prague from the castle is compelling, because of the sweep of uniform, orange hued, tile roofs from the castle wall to the river.

Also from the hilltop, one has the best view of a Prague icon—the Charles Bridge, which is lined with statues and provides a view up and down the river as well as a pedestrian crossing into the Old Town. The Old Town Square has two compelling icons. The first is the large memorial to Jan Hus, who was burned to death for his religious views. The second is the astronomical clock on the Old Town Hall. Southwest of the square is the New Town, the most impressive part of which is Wenceslas Square. Less a square than a boulevard, this street slopes gently downhill from the National Museum toward the river. It is lined with hotels and businesses

with impressive architecture, but it is the brilliantly flowered center of the
street which commands attention because of its colorful displays. Also at
the head of the boulevard is a statue of St. Wenceslas, which has become a
popular meeting place for demonstrations and uprisings.

Fig. 8-9 Old Town Square Prague

While tourists come to Prague for, among other things, its visual
attractiveness, the city is also eminently livable. Like most large cities,
automobile traffic is often congested, but the city is compact enough to
offer easy pedestrian movement facilitated by several areas, such as the
Old Town Square, which are closed to automobiles. Parks and gardens are
plentiful. There is a modest metro system, as well as a more extensive
trolley one. Most parts of the city are reasonably populated by restaurants
and bars. Prague is somewhat reminiscent of Athens as an urban design
with its hilltop fortress, and of course like Paris, London, and Berlin with
its riverside setting.

Poznan, Poland, is both off the main tourist track and something of a
surprise compared to the other visually compelling cities in this chapter.
Nonetheless, it is indeed visually impressive. At one point in its past,
Poznan was a circular, walled city reminiscent of Ancient Athens.

Fig. 8-10 Poznan Town Hall

Although the fortifications around the city have largely been destroyed, the essential layout remains. At the city center is the old town square ringed with businesses, open-air cafés, and the beautiful Town Hall with its mechanical goats, the latter the symbol of the city. Though damaged in World War II, the old town square has had many of its old structures refurbished. Radiating away from this agora-like space is the modern city. Located just off the square is the impressive baroque St. Stanislaus Cathedral. Off the square and up one of the few hills in this part of the city is the National Museum and Raczyński Library, impressive examples of modern and Neoclassical architecture respectively.

On the way north to these structures is the Royal Castle, dating originally to the 13th century, and portions of the wall that once surrounded the city of which it was a part. Also in the area of the National Museum is another Neoclassical building, the Great Theatre or opera house. Facing this theatre is one of Poznan's many small parks with a pond and fountain. North and west of the National Museum is the building known as the Kaiser's Castle. This structure was extensively remodeled during the Nazi era by Hitler's architect, Albert Speer, for use by Adolf Hitler once the war was won by the Nazis. It is an imposing structure but one with bad memories for many Poles. In the boulevard across from this castle are twin crosses memorializing the Polish workers' uprising during the Soviet era.

East of the old town square is Cathedral Island, a site in the River Warta with a number of churches including the Gothic revival Cathedral of St. Peter and St. Paul. North of the town square is the huge Citadel Park, which includes two military museums and a cemetery for soldiers of both World Wars I and II. Poznan is also the home of Adam Mickiewicz

University designed in Dutch Renaissance style. In the eastern part of the city, off the Cybina River is the city zoo. So Poznan, although a small city by comparison to others in this chapter, has all of the features of a visually impressive city: iconic buildings, parks and gardens, restaurants and cafés, and an extensive tram and bus network to make the city easily accessible. Poznan is an important stop on the express train line running from Berlin to Warsaw, putting the city on a main artery of commerce. Partially in acknowledgement of this fact, Poznan was chosen as a host city in 2012 to UEFA championship soccer/football matches. Before moving across the Atlantic Ocean to North America, two more visually compelling European cities will be considered. These are Stockholm, Sweden, and Copenhagen, Denmark.

Fig. 8-11 Skeppsholmen

Stockholm and Copenhagen are unique among the cities of Europe being considered here in that they lie on large bodies of water rather than along rivers. Stockholm lies at the eastern end of Lake Mälaren, with the Baltic Sea on the city's eastern edge. The abundance of water is not the only visually compelling aspect of Stockholm, but it is certainly a significant one. Fully a third of the area within the city limits is made up of water. Another third is parks and woods, so that the character of the city is that of clean air and fresh water. The city is also built on fourteen islands, and an archipelago extending from Stockholm east and north in the Baltic Sea, which includes 24,000 islands (Proctor and Roland 2006). The city dweller in this case, as well as the visitor, has ample opportunities for recreation and sightseeing.

The city center of Stockholm is a very modern one with skyscrapers and an abundance of different businesses lying uphill from the harbor. The story is very different near the harbor. In addition to the ubiquitous cruise ships and private yachts and sailboats, the harbor is ringed by extravagant hotels. The National Art Museum is also located here, and from this spot a bridge takes the visitor to the island of Skeppsholmen. This naturally wooded little island is home to the Modern Art Museum, the Architecture Museum, and the Museum of Far Eastern Antiquities. The National Art Museum has a notable collection of Swedish paintings by Anders Zorn and Carl Larsson, as well as a respectable collection of European masters such as El Greco, Gainsborough, Gauguin, and Renoir. These museums, as well as their settings, are visual icons for Stockholm. Opposite Skeppsholmen on the east is the Vasa Museum, featuring the recovered 17th century warship Vasa, which unfortunately sank in the Stockholm harbor on its maiden voyage.

Fig. 8-12 Gamla Stan

Opposite Skeppsholmen on the west is Gamla Stan, the city's old town, which features many buildings dating to earlier centuries of Stockholm's past. The most prominent of these is undoubtedly the Baroque Royal Palace, dating to the 18th century. Storkyrkan is a church dating originally to the 14th century but remodeled in the 18th century along Baroque lines. Swedish monarchs have married and been crowned here. Gamla Stan has many fine places to eat and a number of hotels, befitting its status as a tourist attraction.

Back on the mainland, just north of Gamla Stan, is the city's principal park, Kungsträdgården. Less a park than an open, paved square lined with trees, this park was once the king's kitchen garden. It is a meeting place for Stockholm residents, a performance venue, and is populated with numerous cafés. Further north and west is the city's train and bus station, with links to Arlanda International Airport outside Stockholm. Transportation within the city makes access to all of Stockholm's principal sites easy. There are bus routes, but the most extensive mode of transportation is the Tunnelbana or metro. Stockholm is also eminently walkable, which makes for easy access anywhere and makes it possible to enjoy the visually compelling sights, the most pleasant of which is the water.

Fig. 8-13 Rosenborg Slot and Gardens

Copenhagen shares Stockholm's attractive natural settings. Also located on a Baltic Sea harbor, the city is laced with canals somewhat suggestive of Venice and has an ample supply of parks and gardens to provide rest, relaxation, and recreation. One of these gardens is Tivoli, an amusement park with rides for both children and adults, carefully tended flower gardens, restaurants, a concert hall, and an aquarium. The city originated on the small island of Slotsholmen, although today there are so many bridges to the little island that it hardly seems to be separate from the mainland at all. Copenhagen's iconic buildings are spread throughout the city, and Slotsholmen is home to Christiansborg Slot or Palace. This early 20th century Baroque structure is now the home of the Prime Minister and the Danish Parliament.

There are many such iconic structures in Copenhagen. Near Slotsholmen and southwest is Ny Carlsberg Glyptotek, with Egyptian and Greek antiquities, 19th and 20th century Danish art, and examples of French Impressionism. Just west of Slotsholmen is the National Museum, Denmark's largest history museum. North of Slotsholmen across central Copenhagen is Rosenborg Castle, home of the Danish Crown Jewels, set in the vast and elegant royal gardens. Adjacent to Rosenborg Castle are the botanical gardens, complete with trees, open lawns, flower gardens, and lakes. Within these gardens is the National Art Gallery, home to Danish art as well as that of the European masters.

East of Rosenborg Slot near the harbor is Amalienborg and Frederiksstaden where stand four Rococo palaces set in an octagonal square. Dating to the mid-18th century, these palaces were originally home to four different aristocratic families but were purchased by the Danish king in 1794 and continue to be the residences of the royal family today. Directly across the harbor from this Rococo splendor is a radically different piece of architecture, the Opera House, which is an ultra-modern building somewhat suggestive in its location and style of the Sydney, Australia, Opera House. Well north along the harbor is the small statue of Hans Christian Andersen's Little Mermaid, which is perhaps not so visually compelling as it is a sentimental tourist attraction.

Copenhagen is, like Stockholm, easily accessible within via train and metro, but it is also very conducive to cycling and walking. Copenhagen's pedestrian shopping mall, Strøget, offers a variety of commercial venues. The train station near Tivoli Gardens links the city with Kastrup International Airport as well as a number of other international destinations. Later in this chapter, other cities set near the sea will also be examined, including Sydney, Australia, and Wellington, New Zealand, which offer further evidence of the visual impressiveness of cities near the water. Now, a city with a wholly different type of visual impressiveness will be examined. It is Québec City, in the Canadian province of Québec, the only walled fortress in North America.

The ancient Athenians sought locations for their cities that gave them a high point from which to see potential enemies coming and to provide for self defense. Once having established the city, the Athenians usually ringed it with walls to make a fortress. Québec City follows these ideas. It was founded in 1608 by Samuel de Champlain as the first major French settlement in Canada. Québec City sits along the St. Lawrence River, and although there is a Lower Town much of the city itself is in the Upper Town on a bluff called Cap Diamant. Walls surround much of the Upper Town, including a walled military installation called the Citadel. It was never necessary to defend the city with military might settled behind the walled fortress, but an active military presence even today is prepared to do so.

Fig. 8-14 Place Royale

Québec City, although it certainly has a number of modern buildings, appeals to the eye first because of the buildings preserved from its past. The lower town, for example, has an entire set of city blocks devoted to the preservation of the old city in the center of which is a plaza called Place Royale. In these old buildings today are restaurants, hotels, and souvenir shops, but the heart of the main square is the Église Notre-Dame-des-Victoires, which dates to 1688. Only steps away is the Musée de la Civilization featuring a number of eclectic exhibits both ancient and modern but focusing on life in Québec. Somewhat north of Place Royale is the Old Port, which today has restaurants as well as points of departure for river tours. Off Place Royale is a funicular leading to the Upper Town.

Fig. 8-15 Parc de l'Esplanade

The funicular delivers visitors to a large plaza fronting the massive Château Frontenac. This beautiful hotel, complete with battlements and turrets, looks more like a castle than a hotel. Parks and gardens both large and small dot the Upper Town. There is a small park just downhill from the hotel called Place d'Armes, which is a gathering place for traveling performers. Uphill from the hotel as one ascends to the top of Cap Diamant is the larger Parc de l'Esplanade. At the hilltop is the Hôtel du Parlement, a chateau where the Québecois "National Assembly" meets. Surrounding this building are extensive flower gardens and fronting it at the street is the massive Fontaine de Tourny.

In terms of architecture, gardens, and water, the pinnacle of the Upper Town is most impressive visually and also provides a panoramic view of the St. Lawrence River and parts of the Lower Town. La Citadelle and the 267 acre Parc des Champs-de-Bataille lie south of the hilltop. On the western edge of this park is the Musée National des Beaux-Arts du Québec. North and downhill from the Château Frontenac is the Basilique

Cathédrale Notre-Dame de Québec dating to 1647. Since it is comparatively small, Québec City is readily accessible on foot, even though some of the walking is uphill and strenuous. Busses make the main streets readily accessible. The city is a most impressive visual experience, especially the view upward from the river side. From this ancient bastion, one would travel south to the most visually compelling city in the United States of America. The island borough of Manhattan surely rivals Paris for the title of the world's most visually impressive city.

Like a discussion of Paris, an account of the visual persuasiveness of Manhattan is daunting for all the visual elements that might legitimately be considered. However, there can be little question that the most significant visual element of Manhattan is the skyline with its many skyscrapers. Such buildings express structural and visual power by their height and overall size, and they command the visitor to look upward to the heavens (Ragsdale 2011). Additionally, some of these buildings are art objects in their own right. The Empire State Building and especially the Chrysler Building are notable examples. As in Paris, the city is replete with museums of all sorts spread throughout the city. The Metropolitan Museum of Art is second only to the Louvre in its size and the quality of its collection and is an elegant art object itself (Ragsdale 2009a). Nearby, the Guggenheim Museum, designed by Frank Lloyd Wright, is a unique structure resembling an inverted ziggurat. Elsewhere in the city, the iconic Museum of Modern Art is the leading modern and contemporary art venue in the world. Smaller specialty art museums dot the city, and the Museum of Natural History has a world class collection of artifacts and a vast range of exhibits.

Although the popular image of Manhattan probably does not include its religious venues, the city is full of iconic cathedrals and churches. Many of these are world class architectural structures, including the Gothic Roman Catholic St. Patrick's Cathedral in midtown and the huge, still unfinished, Gothic Episcopal Cathedral of St. John the Divine in Morningside Heights. The Central Synagogue in midtown is the oldest Jewish house of worship in the city. At midtown, around the area known as Times Square, there is the complex of live performance venues or theatres known collectively as Broadway, which rival those in London for their quality of performances. Complementing the steel and concrete pathways and structures that are the core of Manhattan is the large and lovely English landscape garden known as Central Park.

Although its traffic is often congested and its sidewalks teeming with both travelers and residents, Manhattan is quite livable. Its extensive subway system makes it easy to access all parts of the island as well as its adjacent boroughs such as Queens and the Bronx, and there are restaurants and other forms of eateries literally everywhere. Additionally, the department and specialty stores of Manhattan make it a buyer's destination for visitors from all over the world. These include Macy's and Saks Fifth Avenue to name just two. For sports fans, the five New York City boroughs feature two major league baseball teams, the Yankees and the Mets, two National Football League franchises, the Giants and the Jets (although the two teams share a home stadium in New Jersey), two National Basketball Association teams, the Knicks and the Nets, as well as hockey and soccer/football clubs. Finally, New York City is the home of the US Open Tennis Tournament.

Manhattan is a major transportation hub. Although none is in Manhattan proper, three sizeable airports serve the city. These are John F. Kennedy International Airport, LaGuardia Airport, and Newark, New Jersey's Liberty International Airport. Trains and taxis into the city are abundant. Grand Central Terminal is one of the grandest iconic structures in the world in addition to being a major train station. Penn Station, with its Beaux-Arts architecture, rivals Grand Central in importance if not in visual impressiveness. In almost every way that a city can be visually compelling, Manhattan is. Perhaps more than any other city in the world its visual impression is that of awe, much like the visual experience of such natural wonders as the Grand Canyon. South of Manhattan is another unique US city, a city designed specifically to be the capital of the US. This is the city of monuments, Washington, DC, which is in many ways America's Paris.

The DC in the designation of Washington stands for District of Columbia. The city is not part of any state, although it was derived from territory belonging to both Maryland and Virginia. The location was once a coastal marsh on the Potomac River. It was converted into a livable place by Pierre Charles L'Enfant, an architect familiar with visually impressive European cities such as Paris and Amsterdam, and Andrew Ellicott. It is roughly a square with 10 miles on each side as prescribed by Congress, which is the District's governing body even though it has a mayor. As the seat of the American Federal Government, Washington, DC, is a city replete with iconic governmental structures and the grand architecture that goes with them, including Georgian, Gothic, and Neoclassical. These visually compelling structures include the Capitol, the White House, and the Supreme Court (Ragsdale 2011).

In addition to the iconic governmental buildings, Washington is a city of monuments to the most important events and people in American history. L'Enfant's original design for the District included an approximately one mile avenue leading to the Capitol, analogous to the Champs Élysées, which is now the National Mall. Many of the most important of the city's monuments are located near this grand avenue. At the end of the avenue opposite the Capitol is the Washington Monument, and leading off to the south are the Lincoln Memorial with its reflecting pool, the World War II Memorial, the Vietnam Veterans Memorial, and the Korean War Veterans Memorial. Around the nearby Tidal Basin are the FDR Memorial and the Jefferson Memorial. A stand of Japanese cherry trees, a gift of the government of Japan, lines the banks of the basin.

Lining the National Mall proper are the buildings of the Smithsonian Institution, also among the most iconic structures in America. The National Gallery, the National Archives, the National Air and Space Museum, and the National Museum of Natural History are the most prominent ones of these. As in Paris, smaller museums are located throughout the city. The District also has many churches and synagogues and is home to the Gothic National Cathedral. Although the District itself is not replete with residential space, the adjacent areas of Georgetown, Arlington, Alexandria, and Bethesda have an abundance of homes and apartments.

Transportation in the city can be congested on surface streets, but there is a fine, new metro system that makes the District and its adjacent suburbs easily accessible. The area is served by Reagan National Airport in Arlington, Virginia, and Dulles International Airport in Fairfax and Loudoun Counties, Virginia, west of the District. Venues for the performing arts and sports are also Washington icons. Perhaps among the world's leading performing arts venues is the John F. Kennedy Center on the Potomac. The Washington Redskins represent the National Football League, the Washington Nationals represent professional baseball, and the Washington Wizards the National Basketball Association. Like New York City, Washington also has hockey and soccer teams.

Finally, Washington, DC, is home to several iconic educational institutions. There are Georgetown University, American University, George Washington University, and Howard University to mention only a few. As in most major American cities, the Washington metropolitan area is home to many of the nation's most prominent department stores, shopping malls, and grocery stores. At mid-continent stands America's "second city," as it is often called. This is Chicago, Illinois, located on the banks of Lake Michigan.

Chicago shares Manhattan's visual power with its skyline of skyscrapers and its majestic parks. Like Paris and Berlin, Chicago is an axial city, although the axis is vertical with Michigan Avenue extending from Congress Plaza Drive in the south to the John Hancock Center in the north and including the Magnificent Mile of high-rise buildings. Roughly paralleling Michigan Avenue is Lakeshore Drive along Lake Michigan. The combination of skyscrapers and water is a powerful visual experience. Additionally, the Chicago River parallels the lake for some distance and then branches off horizontally to empty into the lake and divide the city approximately in half.

Within the city center and adjacent sections of downtown Chicago there are numerous visually impressive and iconic structures comparable in many ways to the very best in the world. America's tallest building, the Willis Tower (formerly the Sears Tower) towers over the city center and offers a vast panoramic view of the area from its skydeck. While this building is the tallest in the city, there are large numbers of similar skyscrapers forming a skyline comparable to that of Manhattan. However, Chicago is not missing large green areas right in the heart of the city. Grant Park lies on the shores of Lake Michigan behind the Art Institute of Chicago. This museum is perhaps the most important city museum in the United States, and its collection of Impressionist paintings is unparalleled.

Chicago may, in fact, be reasonably thought of as a city of museums, nearly all of them among the best in the world. In addition to the Art Institute, there are the Adler Planetarium, the Shedd Aquarium, the Museum of Science and Industry, and the Field Museum of Natural History. It is also a city of universities, including the University of Chicago, the University of Illinois at Chicago, Roosevelt University, DePaul University, and Northwestern University to name just the most prominent ones. Chicago is, oddly enough, not a city such as Manhattan to find much prominent church or cathedral architecture, although there are a number of Polish cathedrals like St. Mary of the Angels that are powerful visual structures.

Chicago is a mercantile and financial center but also a city that is home to several storied sports franchises. The Chicago Bears, of the National Football League, and their Soldier Field stadium are one of the oldest professional football teams in America. In baseball, there are the Cubs and the White Sox, and in basketball there are the Chicago Bulls. Getting around in the city, although it is often a congested place, is eased by major expressways and most especially by the partly elevated train line known as the El, whose circuit around the city center defines the principal hotel and commercial center known as the Loop. Amtrak lines arrive and depart from the city, and on the northwest edges of the city is O'Hare International Airport. All the way to the west coast of the US is the last of the American cities to be considered here as examples of visually impressive urban design. This city combines some of the most visually impressive urban elements of other places considered here. It is San Francisco, with bay and waterside elements, massive bridges linking it to other nearby cities, and with hillside elements.

Fig. 8-16 Alamo Square

San Francisco, the "City by the Bay," sits at the end of a peninsula bordered by the Pacific Ocean on the west and San Francisco Bay on the east. The majestic Golden Gate Bridge lies at the junction of these two bodies of water and gives the traveler access to the Marin Headlands and the city of Sausalito. Further east, the Bay Bridge provides access to Oakland and other parts of the bay area. The city itself rises gently but inexorably upward from the water and from its heights gives spectacular views of the water, the areas across the bridges, and the city itself. These combined features are perhaps San Francisco's most impressive visual elements.

Inland, San Francisco is a commercial and financial center replete with its own visually powerful skyline. The most visually prominent structure in this skyline is undoubtedly the Transamerica Pyramid (Ragsdale 2011). The Bank of California, the Bank of America, and the First Interstate

Center are other visually compelling buildings nearby ir the financial center of the city. Many hotels dot the city landscape as well. San Francisco is not merely a collection of high rise buildings however. Within the city's confines there are a number of green spaces as well as residential housing. Alamo Square, for example, and the Queen Anne houses known as "the Painted Ladies" along one of its borders is as visually becoming a space as one is likely to find in any city. While Alamo Square is small and simply park like, there is a much larger green space near Golden Gate Bridge known as Golden Gate Park.

In Golden Gate Park, which is basically an English landscape garden, there are several other iconic city sites. These include the California Academy of Sciences, the M. H. de Young Museum, and the California Palace of the Legion of Honor. Adjacent to the park on the north is the Presidio, formerly a military post and now itself largely a park. Back nearer the city center is the San Francisco Museum of Modern Art, with its small but representative collection of modern and contemporary art objects and traveling exhibitions.

San Francisco is geographically compact enough to make itself easily accessible by walking were it not for the steep hills, but the city, and especially the city center, features cable car lines that not only conquer the hills but make for an amusement park like ride. Transportation is, in general, readily available and includes Bay Area Rapid Transit, busses, and the Muni Metro. To the south of the city proper is San Francisco International Airport. From Fisherman's Wharf and its surrounding areas on the water, one can not only dine on freshly caught seafood but also take a boat to Alcatraz Island in the bay or to various points on land opposite the city.

San Francisco is not without its iconic forms of church and governmental architecture. On Nob Hill, for example, is Grace Cathedral, modeled after Notre-Dame de Paris, and a short walk or ride from the city center is the visually compelling Baroque City Hall, with its dome modeled after St. Peter's in Rome and appearing for all the world like the palace of a European monarch. The city is also the home of the National Football League San Francisco 49ers, the baseball San Francisco Giants, and across the bay in Oakland the National Basketball Association Golden State Warriors, as well as such major universities as the private University of San Francisco and, again across the bay, the University of California, Berkeley. For the final three visually compelling cities to be considered in this chapter, a journey southwestward across the Pacific Ocean from San Francisco is necessary. This journey ends first in Sydney, Australia, but continues on to Melbourne, Australia, and Wellington, New Zealand.

Sydney shares many aspects of visual impressiveness with San Francisco, inasmuch as it is also a city on a harbor. It lacks the San Francisco hills, but there are many other similarities. Also located on a harbor, Melbourne shares San Francisco's hills, and Wellington is also both hilly and on a harbor. It is difficult to know where to start with Sydney, since there are so many visually impressive aspects to the city— the water, the churches, the parks and gardens, the museums, and so on. However, the single most iconic structure in the city is surely the Sydney Opera House, with its distinctive architecture, sitting right on the water in the harbor. This unique building, with its clamshell roofs, is in fact one of the world's greatest pieces of architecture and a visual delight by any measure (Ragsdale 2011). Almost equally iconic are the Sydney Harbor Bridge across the harbor from the Opera House and St. Mary's Cathedral, a Gothic Revival building nearer the city center. In the general area of the harbor, there is a very extensive aquarium and the Museum of Contemporary Art.

Fig. 8-17 Sydney Opera House

Behind the Opera House and leading to the city center are the vast Royal Botanic Gardens and the Domain, considered previously in this book, where the Art Gallery of New South Wales is located (Ragsdale

2011). These two parks lead almost directly to Hyde Park on the edge of the city center. Along nearby Macquarie Street are several architectural icons of the city. These are the State Library of New South Wales, Parliament House, Sydney Hospital, the Mint, Hyde Park Barracks Museum, the Land Titles Office, and St. James Church. These buildings represent a variety of architectural styles from Neoclassical to Georgian to Victorian. In addition to the water of Sydney harbor, there is a large fountain in Hyde Park, and the combination of the greenery of the parks of the city and the water maintain the feel of nature in the otherwise not very natural concrete city canyons.

Much of the Sydney city center is easily walkable and both shops and restaurants abound. However, the city is large enough that public transportation is needed for travel to many other areas. Sydney is blessed in this regard with trams, busses, train, and light rail services that make for easy access. There is also Sydney International Airport. For nearby harbor locations, there is also an extensive system of water taxis and boats leaving from and arriving at Sydney harbor. Sydney's skyline is visually compelling and includes a 1,000 foot tower with an observation deck and restaurant among other features, but surely Sydney's claim to visual persuasiveness is its water, its greenery, and its iconic Opera House. South and west along the coast from Sydney is Australia's "second city," Melbourne. Melbourne sits on Victoria Harbor rather deeply within Port Phillip, which is topographically like a lake.

Melbourne is Australia's second most populous city, after Sydney, and is characterized visually by quite a large number of iconic governmental buildings, cathedrals, museums, and universities. It is also dotted throughout with parks and gardens, which, along with the nearby harbor and the Yarra River running through the southern part of the city, offer the resident and the visitor both an abundance of natural complements to the concrete and steel structures of a modern city.

Swanston Street, running north and south in Melbourne, is a good place to see several of the city's iconic structures. At the upper reaches of the street, one may see the ultra-modern architecture of the Royal Melbourne Institute of Technology as well as the Edwardian city baths. Traveling downhill, one will encounter the massive Neoclassical State Library of Victoria, with its domed reading room. At the bottom of Swanston Street, there is the Gothic Anglican St. Paul's Cathedral diagonally across from the Victorian Flinders Street Station and directly across from Federation Square, a visually dramatic contemporary shopping and entertainment mall.

As it crosses the Yarra River, Swanston Street becomes St. Kilda Road, which takes one past the parks of King's Domain and the Royal Botanic Gardens considered earlier in this book. Just after crossing the river, however, one will find two more of Melbourne's iconic structures. These are the Victorian Arts Center, with its 375 foot spire, and the National Gallery of Victoria. Across the river from the King's Domain are two renowned sporting complexes: Melbourne Cricket Ground and the National Tennis Center, the latter the home of the annual Australian Open Tennis Tournament.

Also on either side of Swanston Street, Melbourne spreads out and is well-populated with its share of modern commercial and financial skyscrapers, including the 58 story Rialto Towers and the Crowne Entertainment Center. East of Swanston Street on Eastern Hill is Melbourne's Parliament area. Here one will find the Renaissance Revival style Treasury Building and the Georgian Parliament House. Eastern Hill is also the home of the Gothic Roman Catholic St. Patrick's Cathedral (Ragsdale 2011) and the lush green Fitzroy Gardens. Just northwest of Eastern Hill is Carlton Gardens, another English landscape style garden, where the very modern Melbourne Museum and the more traditional Neoclassical Royal Exhibition Building are located. Nearby is the University of Melbourne campus.

Although many residents travel to and through the city in their private automobiles, Melbourne has a Metlink system consisting of several bus, tram, and train routes providing comprehensive service to all parts of the city and surrounding areas. Flinders Street Station provides rail service to other parts of Australia, and river boats provide sightseeing tours of the city. Just outside the city is Melbourne International Airport. Not so hilly as San Francisco, the Melbourne city center is quite walkable and at every turn it seems there are interesting visual attractions such as older churches and theaters.

Finally, there is Wellington, the capital of New Zealand, and the southernmost city on the country's North Island. Wellington is rather small, with the city clustered around Lambton Harbor and backed by the hilly remnants of the island's volcanic past. Except for the suburbs, the city is a walking one. As the capital of New Zealand, the economy of Wellington is primarily the product of the government and its services, and indeed many of the city's iconic structures are governmental ones. Especially notable in this regard are three buildings on a hill overlooking the harbor. These are the Neoclassical Parliament Building and its modern so-called Beehive wing and the Gothic Parliamentary Library with their surrounding flower gardens (Ragsdale 2011). Below these buildings toward the harbor is a complex of Old Government Buildings built of wood made to resemble stone. Both the imposing architecture and the hilly location make these governmental structures particularly compelling visually.

Nearby, one also will find the Gothic Cathedral Church of St. Paul, now known as Old St. Paul's, constructed entirely of wood including its nails. Also nearby is the modern Wellington Cathedral of St. Paul. Old St. Paul's is now confined to largely ceremonial occasions such as weddings and funerals. Along the hill to the southeast of the Parliament Building and the cathedrals are Victoria University and Wellington Botanic Garden, the latter of which has been previously discussed in this book. A cable car still functions to carry passengers up the hill from the city below. Overlooking the harbor to the southeast are numerous colorful hilltop homes reminiscent of the Victorian and Queen Anne homes to be found in the Pacific Heights and Alamo Square areas of San Francisco.

Fig. 8-18 Wellington Botanic Garden

Right on the harbor are to be found Queens Wharf, with its shops, restaurants, and bars, and one of the most iconic structures to be found in any city, the Museum of New Zealand/Te Papa Tongarewa. This is a modern omni-museum (Ragsdale 2009b) containing traditional paintings as well as items most often found in a museum of natural history. Wellington, however, is primarily a visually impressive city for its water and its natural greenery, and there are plenty of outdoor cafés which take full advantage of these features. Wellington is the culmination of this examination of cities as examples of visual persuasion, therefore it should be possible to draw some general conclusions about what makes a city visually compelling.

Cities are designed for their residents, and to some extent for their visitors to be sure, but they are not merely utilitarian. City designers also have in mind creating spaces in such a way and with such contents that the result is a persuasive message to others. This message is multifaceted, in that cities are meant to evoke images of power, prestige, status, and beauty. Hence, in every visually compelling city, as is evident, there are iconic structures, such as museums, libraries, governmental buildings, cathedrals, universities, monuments, and memorials. Among other things, these iconic structures argue the premise that this is one of the world's great cities. Although many aspects of urban design are meant to enhance the livability of a city, including readily available housing and transportation, accessible goods and services, and spaces for relaxation and recreation, these aspects also contribute to the overall argument about a city's status and prestige. As noted at the beginning of Chapter One, "Intensely three-dimensional space has the remarkable capacity to enhance our lives. It imparts our surroundings with a pleasing sense of comfort and security that is as important to the enjoyment of life as sunlight and a place to rest. It is a basic component of good urban design" (Hedman & Jaszewski 1984, 53).

CHAPTER NINE

INTERIOR SPACES

The focus of this book has been to this point primarily exterior designed spaces, especially parks and gardens. It is also true, however, that designed space has always been an essential part of great architecture. With that fact in mind, therefore, this penultimate chapter will consider several visually compelling interior designed spaces in order to understand their persuasive power. In modern times, a particularly important example of the design of space to influence visitors may be found in the various shopping malls around the world. Two of these, the Mall of America in Minneapolis, Minnesota, and the Dubai Mall in Dubai, United Arab Emirates, will serve to illustrate the power of designed space to influence visitors and to shape buying habits. The great examples of architecture from earlier times have also influenced visitors and shaped behaviors within their walls, although not usually for commercial purposes. Cathedrals, such as Notre Dame de Paris, St. Peter's, Salisbury, Yorkminster, Liverpool, the Pantheon, and St. Paul's, have profoundly influenced parishioners as well as those who have come to them just to marvel. Government buildings, like the Reichstag and the US Capitol, were similarly designed to overwhelm the visitor with their interior power. Museums, such as the Metropolitan Museum of Art and the British Museum, performance halls, such as the Opéra Garnier, and chapels, such as the Sistine Chapel, all affect visitors with their compelling form. In the following pages, such structures as these will be examined for how their interior design features contribute to visual impressiveness.

Shopping Malls

Precursors of today's shopping mall date well into antiquity and include Rome's ancient Trajan's Market, and throughout the world there are examples of collections of shops constituting shopping streets or centers. In America, shopping centers date to the 1920s in California (Feinberg and Meoli 1991). Not merely commercial centers, these shopping areas were also intended to be places for socializing. Modern shopping malls, however, probably share their origin with the sharp rise of suburban living in the United States following World War II. As cities increased their sizes and populations, especially after the return of service men and women at the end of the war, living spaces became scarce and, as a result, expensive, both of which results contributed to the development of residential areas outside cities. Also contributing to the expansion of suburbs in America even before the war was the development of transportation from the simple horse and rider sort to horse drawn carriages to trains to busses and to automobiles. Although early forms of mass transportation made cities accessible from suburbs for those who worked in urban areas, it was still necessary to provide commercial services within suburbs that were more easily and readily accessible and, as noted above, to provide a kind of community center to bring suburban residents into contact with each other. Although shopping malls may be found throughout the United States, perhaps the quintessential mall is Minnesota's Mall of America. Not only is it the largest shopping center in America, this mall also illustrates the varieties of features used to influence visitors.

The Southdale Center in Edina, Minnesota, which opened in 1956, was the first enclosed shopping center and the nearest precursor to the Mall of America in Bloomington, Minnesota, near Minneapolis and St. Paul, which opened in 1992 (http://www.simon.com). The Mall of America offered 4.2 million square feet of space on four levels at its opening, and today it is in the process of a major expansion. It added large-scale entertainment to the usual cinema complexes to be found in most malls with a walk-through aquarium, a seven acre amusement park including a Ferris wheel and a roller coaster, and night clubs for adult entertainment (http://www.mallofamerica.com).

Around the world, there is obviously a competition for who has the largest and most diverse mall, much like the competition for the world's tallest building. In 2005, the Mall of the Emirates opened in Dubai, United Arab Emirates, with 450 retailers, 70 restaurants, and indoor snow skiing with five runs and two sliding hills. This complex is 25 stories high and attracts 1,500 guests a day. Those who wish to stay longer have the option of accommodations at a hotel with chalet-type suites (http://www.mallof theemirates.com). In spite of its size and offerings, the Mall of the Emirates is by no means the only one in Dubai. Ibn Battuta Mall emphasizes culture and history in the design of its interiors in what amounts to a theme park covering 3.1 million square feet on one level (http://www.ibnbattutamall.com). Dubai Festival City is a large retail, residential, and business complex containing malls as well as apartments and hotels (http://www.dubaifestivalcity.com).

Clearly, malls offer much more than retail outlets, and visiting a mall is part of the lifestyle of many people. Young people in America flock to malls to meet others and to find entertainment. Older people often use a mall's open spaces to get a bit of exercise, a practice known as "mall-walking." Mall space is designed to accomplish several goals, all of which have to do with exerting influence over visitors.

First, mall space is designed to attract visitors in the first place. Some visitors come initially to dine but stay for the mall's other attractions. Malls encourage visitors to stay longer than the time it would take simply to make a few purchases. Entertainment and restaurants foster longer stays, and the longer the stay the more likely visitors are to spend. Malls also need clean, crisp sight lines and open, skylighted spaces to make the shops and other offerings visible and accessible. These sight lines translate into broad pathways leading to various shops. Shop owners, of course, vie for positions near entryways, restaurants, and entertainment venues so as to attract customers who do not come especially to shop. While one might not be readily aware of the many ways mall designers seek to influence a visit, it is nonetheless true that visiting a mall is subjecting oneself to substantial visual persuasion. Although radically different in a number of ways from shopping malls, cathedrals are also designed so that their interior spaces powerfully impact their visitors.

Cathedrals

Cathedrals as visually persuasive structures have been examined extensively elsewhere (Ragsdale 2007, 2011), so it is the purpose of the examples in this chapter to illustrate both typical and especially notable instances of interior design. In many of the world's great cathedrals, the layout of the interior was in the form of the Christian cross. Not only did this cruciform layout carry powerful symbolic meaning, it also served to lead the visitor inexorably through the nave to the altar beyond the transept. Especially in the great Gothic churches, massive windows to allow light to penetrate the cathedral were extremely important. The windows themselves were usually made of stained glass depicting Biblical scenes and scenes of local interest. The light coming in was therefore brilliantly colored in reds, greens, blues, yellows, and the like. Light was seen as a means by which God revealed himself to Humankind (Scott 2005). As a result, cathedral interiors in general and not just Gothic ones were to be seen symbolically as earthly examples of life in Heaven. Light, however, was not the only aspect of a cathedral interior to represent the

Fig. 9-1 York Minster

Heavenly City. Enormous size and the sheer mass of open space complemented the brilliance of light. Size and open space together suggest the vastness of Heaven and perhaps the degree to which it is all-encompassing. Lining the open space of the nave were massive stone columns supporting the roof vaulting, and typically these columns as well as the vaulting were gracefully designed and rhythmically repeated. Finally, cathedral interior spaces were often colorfully painted and gilded as well as adorned with paintings and sculpture. Heaven has been described as being paved with streets of gold, which may account for the colorful ornamentation of cathedral interiors (Revelation 21:21).

The largest Gothic cathedral in Europe is York Minster in the walled city of York in northern England. The Minster interior is quite large and is brightly illuminated by 128 stained glass windows. Clustered Corinthian columns along the length of the nave are topped with peaked arches, and above these there are two additional levels of arched stained glass windows. The ceiling featuring ribbed vaulting is white and adorned with gilded and painted medallions at the intersections of the ribs (http://www.yorkminster.org). The Great East Window, built in the early 15th century by master glazier John Thornton, is larger than a tennis court with 117 panels depicting the Creation, Old Testament scenes, and the

Fig. 9-2 York Minster Choir Screen

events of the biblical book of Revelation (Hampson 2005). Finally, the Choir Screen is made of white stone and features 15 statues of English kings. The pedestals of each statue are gilded, as are the ornaments above each of them, and the entryway to the choir has a gilded peaked arch. It is not hard to understand the message that to visit York Minster is to taste a bit of what Heaven will be like.

Salisbury Cathedral, located southwest of London in the small town of the same name, is notable for having the tallest spire in England at 404 feet (http://www.salisburycathedral.org.uk). It is also set in the largest cathedral close in the country. While the cathedral exterior is certainly visually compelling, the interior of the cathedral is perhaps even more powerful. Its scale is especially large in the vertical dimension. Along the sides of the nave and behind the choir stained glass windows illuminate and color the interior. Clustered Doric columns connected by repeated peaked arches line the nave and provide a harmonious visual rhythm. Two tiers of shorter columns and arches separated by windows rises above these, and the vaulting of the ceiling is ribbed.

There are two cathedrals in Liverpool, United Kingdom, whose interior spaces are especially compelling visually. Both are comparatively new, having been constructed in the 20th century. Liverpool Cathedral,

Fig. 9-3 Salisbury

completed in 1978, is the largest Anglican cathedral in the UK and Europe as well (http://www.tripadvisor.com). Liverpool Metropolitan Cathedral of Christ the King is a Catholic cathedral of modern architectural design completed in 1967 (http://www.liverpoolmetrocathedral.org.uk). The nave of the Anglican cathedral, known as the well, is sunken, which has the effect of magnifying the already large size of the interior space of the building (http://www.liverpoolcathedral.org.uk). Indeed, it is the vertical dimension of the space that is the most awe-inspiring in this church. The role of large cathedral space as a means of visual persuasion is captured in the cathedral website's comment that "the central space dominates your view of the Cathedral and its enormity gives an impression of the Cathedral architect's vision of our relationship with God." The cathedral, like others, is replete with art, sculpture, and stained glass windows.

The Liverpool Metropolitan Cathedral of Christ the King has a modern design that sets it apart from most other cathedrals in the UK if not the world. The exterior, viewed from some distance, resembles a helmet of sorts or perhaps a crown. Its vertical walls at ground level form a circle whereupon there is a conical structure adorned at its pinnacle by another circle of spires. The shape of the building results in an unusual interior design as well. The high altar is in the center of the circular space, and the

Fig. 9-4 Liverpool Cathedral

stained glass, primarily blue, makes the interior especially bright. There is more stained glass in this cathedral than in any other in the United Kingdom or Europe (http://www.bbc.co.uk/history/british).

In London, there are several architecturally notable churches and cathedrals, including Westminster Abbey and the Church of St. Martin-in-the-Fields. Both are located in prime locations with the Abbey near the Palace of Westminster, the seat of government in the UK, and St. Martin-in-the-Fields on one side of Trafalgar Square. Perhaps the most notable cathedral in terms of interior design, however, is St. Paul's, because of the space under its dome. The size of this dome is second only to St. Peter's in the Vatican (http://www.sacred-destinations.com). The arches at the sides of the nave are white with gold capitals. The ceilings and the dome interior are adorned with paintings and gilt. The choir has intricately designed metal gates. The gallery below the dome is called "the whispering gallery," because a person whispering at the wall on one side can be heard by someone on the opposite side the circle is so geometrically perfect.

Notre Dame de Paris may well be the world's most famous Gothic cathedral. It is certainly one of the most visited. Its stained glass windows feature a gallery of images. The rose window in the northern transept has images from the Old Testament, with the center icon exhibiting Mary with

Fig. 9-5 Liverpool Metropolitan Cathedral

the Christ child. The western rose window has varied figures along with calendar references. The choir enclosure has a painted and gilded wooden frieze depicting events in the lives of Mary and Jesus. Elsewhere, the frieze depicts the appearances of Christ following his resurrection. In spite of the numerous stained glass windows, the interior of Notre Dame de Paris is not so well lighted as are the interiors of such modern cathedrals as the Liverpool Metropolitan Cathedral. While not so spacious as, say, York Minster, the interior is nonetheless evocative of the vast space that connotes the Heavenly City.

St. Peter's Basilica in the Vatican has the largest interior of any Christian church in the world. There are even marks on the basilica's floor indicating where some other large cathedrals would fit. This vast interior is richly painted and gilded on all sides and in its dome and is the location of numerous precious works of art such as Michelangelo's *Pietá*. Constructed above the altar and directly under the dome of the cathedral is Gian Lorenzo Bernini's baldacchino, a bronze canopy with twisting columns at each of its corners which rises nearly ten stories from the cathedral floor. In spite of its great size, the interior of St. Peter's unfortunately seems cluttered with statues and works of art, and even with its many windows it is darker within than one might expect. Size, in this case therefore, is the cathedral's most visually compelling feature.

Fig. 9-6 St. Peter's and Bernini's Canopy

The most visually compelling domed building in the city of Rome itself is the Pantheon, rebuilt by the Emperor Hadrian in the 1st century CE. The Pantheon is a large, single-roomed space originally built as a generic temple in honor of all gods and has been used as a governmental building as well as a church. The dome itself is made of Roman concrete with an opening at its peak called an oculus or eye. This opening is 30 feet wide and provides the only illumination for the interior other than the light coming from the building's entrance. The illumination of the interior changes during the day as the location of the sun changes in the sky above. Openings in the floor carry away any rain water that might enter through the oculus. Below and radiating away from the oculus are successive rings of concrete coffers or recessed panels originally containing bronze rosettes depicting the stars of heaven. Niches around the walls of the interior once held statues of Roman gods. The walls are decorated with bronze and multicolored marble, with a floor of marble, granite, and porphyry (Strickland 2001).

Those familiar with World War II history will remember that the city of Dresden, Germany, was the target of firebombing by both British and American bombers in the waning days of the war. In addition to ordinary bombs, incendiary bombs were dropped on the city, which had the effect of creating a firestorm with extremely high temperatures. Destruction and

Fig. 9-7 Pantheon

loss of life in the city was extensive, with much of the city center destroyed. Sometimes referred to as Florence on the Elbe, Dresden was the home of numerous architectural masterpieces, including the Lutheran Frauenkirche. This church imploded from the high temperatures of the firestorm and remained a pile of rubble throughout most of the so-called Cold War, probably because of its location in pre-unification East Germany. However, the church was completely restored with largely private funds and reopened in 2005. Its Baroque interior is a single domed room as in Rome's Pantheon. Its white walls and columns are adorned with statues and gold decoration and complemented by dark wood trim. The area behind the altar has fluted Corinthian columns with gold capitals, statuary, and organ pipes crowning all. The sanctuary has three levels of balconies with brightly painted fronts and columns supporting them. Eight scenes from biblical stories are painted on the inside of the dome. Although some regard the Baroque style as too ornate, it is hard not to see the interior of the Frauenkirche as powerfully compelling visually and an earthly analog of the Heavenly City.

Fig. 9-8 Dresden Frauenkirche

Although there are several notable examples of cathedral architecture interiors in North America, there is perhaps none more impressive in its own way than the cathedral of Notre Dame de Montreal in Canada. There are a number of features which make the interior of this Gothic Revival cathedral visually compelling. There are many religious statues carved from oak and scattered about the nave and altar. Behind and above the altar, the windows are blue and accentuate the light coming into the building from outside. Around these spaces, there is considerable gilt, so that the interior seems to glow with a golden hue. The gold is also accented by brilliant reds, greens, purples, and azures. The interior, like that of the Sistine Chapel to be discussed below, comes very close to being overly ornate, but there is no mistaking its power to inspire visually.

Government Buildings

Government buildings are in many ways like cathedrals in their use of designed space. While their spaces are not intended to suggest the nature of the Heavenly City, government buildings are also usually built on a grand scale inasmuch as size also connotes power and authority. Many, if not all, government buildings are also significant examples of architectural design, as illustrated by the United Kingdom's Palace of Westminster (Ragsdale 2011). This tradition extends from federal government buildings down to state and even local ones. Two federal government buildings in

Fig. 9-9 Reichstag Dome Interior

particular illustrate how interior spaces can be designed to have extreme visual power in conveying the messages of power and authority. These are the German Reichstag building and the US Capitol building.

In today's unified Germany, the German parliament or Bundestag meets in Berlin in the refurbished Reichstag building near the Brandenburg Gate and the line along which ran the former Berlin Wall. The building dates to the last decade of the 19th century and was intended to be the meeting place for the German governing body of the time. It was heavily damaged by arson in 1933 and by Allied bombs during World War II. The Reichstag was a ruin in the years following the war but was never razed. With the reunification of German in 1990, a plan was initiated to restore the Reichstag so that the Bundestag could meet there. Although the building was restored, the dome which was at its center was replaced with a glass and steel structure that has great visual power.

Designed by the British architect, Sir Norman Foster, the new dome has become a major tourist attraction in Berlin and offers a variety of visual experiences for the visitor. The dome itself is a glass structure in a steel framework and contains within a sloping walkway leading up to the top and down. The interior of the dome is visually impressive in itself, but the 360° view of the surrounding city is quite compelling. Virtually every significant landmark in the city, from the Tiergarten to the Television Tower to the Brandenburg Gate, is visible as one encircles the interior of the dome. The dome's center is another glass and steel framework structure in the form of an inverted cone which permits one to look down into the working areas of the Bundestag itself. Around the perimeter of the central cone is a steel barricade with imprints of significant dates in the history of Berlin.

Fig. 9-10 US Capitol Rotunda Dome

The US Capitol is one of the world's most familiar landmarks, although its interior is much less visited. On the second floor, one finds the Capitol rotunda lying directly beneath the building's dome, a space reminiscent of the interior of Rome's Pantheon. This visually impressive space has been the location of the lying in state of deceased Presidents and is encircled by statues of former Presidents. In the eye of the dome is a fresco entitled the Apotheosis of Washington in which the first President is depicted ascending into Heaven. Encircling the fresco are stars set within circles, and below this ring are a series of medallions within squares set above windows that ring the dome and are framed by exterior columns. At the base of the dome is a frieze depicting scenes from American history.

The walls of the rotunda feature paintings. The dominant colors are white, beige, and gold, and the interior is bathed with light from the windows much as a Gothic cathedral interior is.

Government building interiors, like the buildings in which they are found, seem intended to convey visually the trappings of authority and power through the elements of space, size, color, and light. They are meant to impress visitors visually. Similarly, great art museums complement their exterior design and the quality and quantity of their collections with temple-like spaces within. These temples of the muses, as they have been called (Ragsdale 2011), provide gallery spaces for the display of their collections but do not neglect to impress the visitor visually with their formidable entrance spaces. There are numerous examples of such interiors both in the US (Ragsdale 2009a) and in Europe (Ragsdale 2009b), but two examples come especially to mind with respect to awe-inspiring entrance spaces. These are the Grand Court of the British Museum in London and the entrance rotunda of the Metropolitan Museum of Art in Manhattan.

Museums

Fig. 9-11 British Museum Grand Court

In the original design of the British Museum, there was a two-acre interior courtyard intended to be a garden. Including a garden may well have been part of the English tradition of public gardens discussed previously in this book. By the mid-19th century, however, a building was erected in the courtyard to house the museum's library holdings, and the space for the garden was lost. In 1997, these library holdings were moved to the new British Library in St. Pancras making it possible to reopen the courtyard to the public. For this purpose, Sir Norman Foster, who redesigned the Reichstag as noted above, received a contract to redesign the courtyard which he did in a fashion similar to the Berlin building. He covered the courtyard with a glass and steel canopy consisting of 3,312 panes of glass with no two being alike. The idea was to present the viewer with a new view at each turn in walking through the highly illuminated courtyard (http://www.britishmuseum.org). The center of the courtyard was the location of the library stacks, which has now been enclosed by a circular building housing the museum's reading room. The visual impression is one of airy lightness, high illumination, and plentiful spaciousness.

The Metropolitan Museum of Art stands on the edge of Central Park along Fifth Avenue in Manhattan. It is a huge building housing a collection of art objects second only in size to that of the Louvre. The museum's galleries are many, but they are no more remarkable visually than those in many of the world's great art museums. However, the entrance rotunda of the museum is highly compelling visually. Its domed ceilings rise two stories above the main floor above large arches. The spacious room also has brilliant window illumination, offering an unmistakable sense of awe. This interior is a dramatic introduction to the visual attractions of this largest US art museum.

The Sistine Chapel and Versailles' Hall of Mirrors

Two other structures deserve consideration in this account of notable interior designs, although neither of them fits into one of the categories above. They are the Sistine Chapel, adjacent to St. Peter's Basilica in Vatican City, and the Hall of Mirrors in Louis XIV's palace at Versailles, France. The Sistine Chapel is a rectangular building with few special adornments on the exterior. There are no external entrances. Entrances are all from within other adjacent buildings. Built in the 15th century as one of the places of worship of the apostolic palace, the most notable function of the chapel today is the meeting place of papal conclaves convened to choose a new Pope. The building is a simple rectangle whose interior dimensions are the same as those given in the Old Testament for the Temple of Solomon (Mancinelli 1993). In arguments about the most beautiful and visually compelling interiors in the world, the Sistine Chapel is easily among the most familiar candidates. Its walls are adorned with original works by the leading painters of the day, with the barrel vaulted ceiling and the wall behind the altar frescoed with perhaps Michelangelo's most famous works.

From ground level looking upward, there are three sections or tiers of paintings on the wall surfaces of the Sistine Chapel. On these surfaces, one will find works by Sandro Botticelli, Perugino, and Domenico Ghirlandaio among others depicting biblical scenes. The ceiling frescoes by Michelangelo depict creation scenes from the biblical book of Genesis, the most famous of which is the Creation of Adam. The banishment from Eden, Noah and the flood, and David and Goliath are a few of the other stories of which there are 39 in all. Following the completion of the ceiling, Michelangelo was commissioned to paint the wall behind the altar showing the Last Judgment. Not only is the ceiling and altar wall work compelling in its size, it is also beautifully colorful.

Fig. 9-12 Hall of Mirrors

Although secular, the Hall of Mirrors in Louis XIV's palace at Versailles, France, is no less visually impressive than the interior of the Sistine Chapel. Like the chapel ceiling, the Hall of Mirrors ceiling is barrel vaulted and covered with numerous large and small paintings depicting the king in various historical moments and separated with gilded frames and ornamental carvings. Down the length of the hall hang enormous chandeliers both along the center as well as the sides of the space. Gold statues holding crystal candelabra range along the length of the hall on either side of every window. There are 17 windows looking out over portions of the Versailles gardens and across the hall from each of these windows are 17 arches each containing 21 mirrors. The combination of light, reflected light, gilt, statuary, and elaborate painting make the hall enormously opulent. The effect is extravagant, but there is no denying its visual power.

The interior spaces discussed here are merely a few of the innumerable ones which might be chosen for study. They are, however, representative of the conclusion that architects pay equally careful attention to the interiors of their buildings as they do to the exteriors. The interior spaces chosen for discussion here also represent quite a range of building types from commercial malls to cathedrals to museums. As such, they support the conclusion that a desire to influence visitors visually pervades the efforts of architectural design.

CHAPTER TEN

REFLECTIONS ON THE VISUAL
PERSUASIVENESS OF STRUCTURES
AND SPACES

This book is the culmination of an effort to examine several visual means of persuasion. There was no thought at the outset that the effort would result in a series of books, yet the outcome is that it did in fact become a logical progression. The first book, *Structures as Argument* (2007), laid the groundwork by demonstrating that a variety of physical structures, such as museums, cathedrals, churches, and the like, were designed with the result in mind of profoundly affecting the attitudes and behaviors, as well as perhaps the beliefs and values, of those who encountered them visually. It was found that structures often incorporated both discursive and nondiscursive elements of persuasion. Cathedrals, for example, featured stained glass depictions of biblical stories and portal sculptures of figures and events from scripture that unfolded like sentences in verbal persuasion and thus were discursive. They also contained regularly repeated visual design elements, such as arched windows and flying buttresses, which impacted viewers visually at a more abstract level and were nondiscursive. It was also found that the distinction between central and peripheral information processing was a useful concept which paralleled the discursive and nondiscursive contrast. Central information processing required the active engagement of cognition to assess facts, examples, and logical connections, while peripheral processing was rather more immediate and non-judgmental.

The first book also introduced the concept of visual semiology as an important way to classify and understand visual signs. Icons were used to classify signs which were clearly representative of what they stood for, such as a painting of the Madonna might be. Indexes, by contrast, not only were clearly representative of what they stood for but were direct evidence of the physical reality of that referent as an unaltered photograph would be. Included in the exposition of icons and indexes was the notion of syntactic indeterminacy by which is meant the associations suggested by the juxtaposition of two or more visual signs. This visual semiology offered an enlightening way of seeing how signs work to influence viewers' perceptions.

The second book, *American Museums and the Persuasive Impulse* (2009a), argued that art museums served a persuasive purpose just as much as they did an educational or preservation one, that the very establishment of a museum is a persuasive act. In this volume, the icon and index semiology referred to above was expanded to include two more visual signs: the symbol and the presentation. It was necessary to include symbols to account for the many visual signs, especially paintings, which incorporated symbolic elements, as in the case of Hieronymus Bosch's *Garden of Earthly Delights*. This painting is neither an icon nor an index but a symbol. Presentations are visual signs that are non-representational as in the case of the majority of modern and contemporary art works. Presentations depend on the visual impact of such elements of abstract art as line, shape, color, mass, and the like.

The second book approached the assessment of American art museums as visual persuasion by examining three aspects of each of a wide variety of institutions. First, it examined the collection of the museum, since museum directors make a concerted effort to acquire a wide variety of art objects as well as distinctive major works. Both of these efforts, at least in part, have as their purpose establishing the museum as a cultural influence or means of visual persuasion. Second, it examined the gallery displays of the museums' collections. Displays are carefully imagined and realized in an effort to influence viewers' visual perceptions of art collections. Third, the book examined the museum building itself as a work of art and a means of pure visual persuasion. Museum buildings are "temples of the muses" and are designed to have a compelling visual effect in and of themselves on visitors.

The third book, *Western European Museums and Visual Persuasion* (2009b) extended the approach of *American Museums* to the great art museums of Western Europe. Finally, *Compelling Form* (2011) considered architecture in general as a means of visual persuasion, expanding the idea of the visual impact of buildings themselves introduced in *Structures as Argument* and incorporated into the assessments of *American Museums* and *Western European Museums*. *Compelling Form* approached the assessment of the visual persuasiveness of buildings with what the author termed the elemental approach. This approach examined the ways in which the elements of graphic design and of architecture, such as line, shape, rhythm, mass, texture, color, and the like, are used as building blocks to create the great museums, cathedrals, government buildings, universities, and so on throughout the Western world.

With the completion of *Compelling Form,* it became clear that there was a missing ingredient in the account of structures as visual persuasion, and that ingredient was designed space. All buildings, for example, contain space, and that space just like the structure itself is arranged for the best use by the building which contains it. Moreover, most buildings are surrounded to a greater or lesser degree by exterior designed spaces which function to extend the visual influence of the building beyond the confines of its walls. Finally, it is clear even to the casual observer that such designed spaces as parks and gardens are so commonplace throughout the civilized world as to be evidence of a human cultural characteristic if not an innate desire.

The present book, therefore, was obviously a natural, perhaps even necessary, extension of the previous four works. It was both appropriate and easy to use the elemental approach for the assessment of visual persuasion through designed spaces, and several general findings are appropriate to summarize here. Pleasure gardens, to use the term in its most general sense, were like museums in that one of their primary purposes was to impress others with the wealth and power of their owners. To be sure, such gardens were thought of like art objects with aesthetic purposes as their goal. In keeping with that aesthetic purpose, pleasure gardens were used as places of retreat from the stresses of everyday work and as places to entertain and to socialize with the owner's guests.

Pleasure gardens became part of the landscape of wealthy owners' property and a natural adjunct to mansions, chateaus, castles, and houses. From this germ of an idea there developed the vast and carefully designed city parks which dot the globe and which function for the general public much as the original pleasure gardens did for the wealthy and influential. National parks, while not actually designed spaces in the same sense as pleasure gardens are, also fulfill these needs and serve in most respects as icons of a country's environmental wealth and prestige. Populating pleasure gardens with both domestic and wild animals became common early on and eventually developed into today's zoological gardens and safari parks. Amusement parks, theme parks, and even modern shopping malls, are further extensions of the pleasure garden concept and serve the same basic needs along with entertainment and commercial enterprise. Theme parks are perhaps the ultimate pleasure gardens, in that they whisk the visitor to another, albeit fantasy, world entirely.

Cities themselves use visual design elements to make both residents and visitors more comfortable in their settings and to make for more livable places. Such concern for visual elements may be seen not only in contemporary cities such as Paris and Berlin but also in ancient ones such as Athens and Rome. Even in the construction of battlefield memorials and cemeteries and battlefield monuments, there seems to be a human bent toward providing something on the order of a pleasure garden. This is not only to memorialize those who have died but also to give the living a sense of visual aesthetics during a visit. As noted in the very beginning of this book, it is relevant again to say that "intensely three-dimensional space has the remarkable capacity to enhance our lives. It imparts our surroundings with a pleasing sense of comfort and security that is as important to the enjoyment of life as sunlight and a place to rest" (Hedman & Jaszewski 1984, 53).

REFERENCES

A View on Cities. Home. http://www.aviewoncities.com.

About.com. Home. http://www.about.com.

Adams, J. A. 1991. *The American amusement park industry: A history of technology and thrills.* Boston: Twayne Publishers.

American Battlefield Monuments Commission. Home. http://www.abmc.gov.

Amsterdam.info. Home. http://www.amsterdam.info.

Aristotle. 1954. *Rhetoric.* Trans. W. R. Roberts. New York: The Modern Library.

Balboa Park. Home. http://www.balboapark.org.

Baratay, E., and E. Hardouin-Fugier. 2002. *Zoo: A history of zoological gardens in the West.* Trans. O. Welsh. London: Reaktion Books Ltd.

BBC. Home. http://www.bbc.co.uk.

Bellingrath Gardens. Home. http://www.bellingrath.org.

Benson, T. W. 2008. Afterword: Look rhetoric! In *Visual rhetoric: A reader in communication and American culture,* ed. L. C. Olson, C. Finnegan, and D. S. Hope, 413-416. Los Angeles: Sage.

Berlin Zoo. Home. http://www.berlin.de.

Boults, E., and C. Sullivan. 2010. *Illustrated history of landscape design.* Hoboken, NJ: John Wiley.

British Museum. Home. http://www.britishmuseum.org.

Buchler, J., ed. 1955. *Philosophical writings of Peirce.* New York: Dover Publications.

Burke, K. 1955. *A rhetoric of motives.* New York: George Braziller.

Cassirer, E. 1955. *The philosophy of the Enlightenment.* Trans. F. C. A. Koelln and J. P. Pettegrove. Boston: Beacon Press.

Central Park. Home. http://www.centralpark.com.

City of London. Home. http://www.cityoflondon.gov.uk.

Ching, F. D. K. 1979. *Architecture: Form, space, & order.* New York: Van Nostrand Reinhold Company.

Cook, D. A. 1996. *A history of narrative film,* 3rd Ed. New York: W. W. Norton.

Discover Los Angeles. Home. http://www.discoverlosangeles.com.

Dondis, D. A. 1973. *A primer of visual literacy.* Cambridge, MA: MIT Press.

Dubai Festival City. Home. http://www.dubaifestivalcity.com.

Dublin Zoo. Home. http://www.dublinzoo.ie.

Duncan, D., and K. Burns. 2009. *The national parks: America's best idea: An illustrated history.* New York: A. A. Knopf.

Eco, U., ed. 2004. *History of beauty.* Trans. A. McEwen. New York: Rizzoli.

Edwards, J. L. 2004. Echoes of Camelot: How images construct cultural memory through rhetorical framing. In *Defining visual rhetorics,* ed. C. A. Hill and M. Helmers, 179-194. Mahwah, NJ: Lawrence Erlbaum.

Feinberg, R. A., and J. Meoli. 1991. A brief history of the mall. *Advances in Consumer Research, 18,* 426-427.

Frost, W., ed. 2011. *Zoos and tourism: Conservation, education, entertainment?* Bristol, UK: Channel View Publications.

Gass, R. H., and J. S. Seiter. 2014. *Persuasion: Social influence and compliance gaining,* 5th Ed. Boston: Pearson.

Gilbert, S., and M. Brouse. 2006. *National Geographic Traveler: Rome,* 2nd Ed. Washington, DC: National Geographic Society.

Hampson, L. 2005. *York Minster.* Norwich, UK: Jarrold Publishing.

Hedman, R., and A. Jaszewski. 1984. *Fundamentals of urban design.* Chicago: American Planning Association.

Hill, C. A. and M. Helmers, eds. 2004. *Defining visual rhetorics.* Mahwah, NJ: Lawrence Erlbaum.

History Learning Site. Home. http://www.historylearningsite.co.uk.

Huntington Gardens. Home. http://www.huntington.org.

Ibn Battuta Mall. Home. http://www.ibnbattutamall.com.

Jones, C. 2005. *Paris: Biography of a city.* New York: Viking.

Kostelnick, C., and M. Hassett. 2003. *Shaping information: The rhetoric of visual conventions.* Carbondale, IL: Southern Illinois University Press.

Lamp, K. S. 2011. "A city of brick": Visual rhetoric in Roman rhetorical theory and practice. *Philosophy and Rhetoric, 44,* 171-193.

Leu Gardens. Home. http://www.leugardens.org.

Lauer, I. 2004. Ritual and power in imperial Roman rhetoric. *Quarterly Journal of Speech, 90,* 422-45.

Liverpool Cathedral. Home. http://www.liverpoolcathedral.org.uk.

Lukas, S. 2008. *Theme park.* London: Reaktion Books.

Mairie de Paris. Home. http://www.paris.fr.

Mall of America. Home. http://www.mallofamerica.com.

Mall of the Emirates. Home. www.malloftheemirates.com.

Mancinelli, F. 1993. *The Sistine Chapel.* Trans. H. McConnachie. Vatican City: Musei Vaticani.

Mémorial de Verdun. Home. http://memorialdeverdun.fr.

Messaris, P. 1997. *Visual persuasion: The role of images in advertising.* Thousand Oaks, CA: Sage.

Metropolitan Cathedral of Christ the King Liverpool. Home. http://www.liverpoolmetrocathedral.org.uk.

Muenchen.de. Home. http://www.muenchen.de.

National Park Service. Home. http://www.nps.gov.

Newhouse, E. L., ed., 1997. *National Geographic's guide to the national parks of the United States,* 3rd Ed. Washington, DC: National Geographic Society.

Oh Ranger.com. Home. http://www.ohranger.com.

Olson, L. C., C. A. Finnegan, and D. S. Hope. 2008. *Visual rhetoric: A reader in communication and American culture.* Los Angeles: Sage.

Osgood, C. E., G. J. Suci, and P. H. Tannenbaum. 1957. *The measurement of meaning.* Urbana, IL: University of Illinois Press.

Petty, R. E., and J. T. Cacioppo. 1986. The Elaboration Likelihood Model of persuasion. In *Advances in experimental social psychology,* ed. L. Berkowitz, 19:123-205. New York: Academic Press.

Prelli, L. J., ed. 2006. *Rhetorics of display.* Columbia, SC University of South Carolina Press.

Prelli, L. J. 2006. Rhetorics of display: An introduction. In *Rhetorics of display,* ed. L. J. Prelli, 1-38. Columbia, SC: University of South Carolina Press.

Proctor, J., and N. Roland. 2006. *The rough guide to Sweden,* 4th Ed. New York: Rough Guides.

Quest-Ritson, C. 2003. *The English garden: A social history.* Jaffrey, NH: David R. Godine.

Ragsdale, J. D., ed. 2007. *Structures as argument: The visual persuasiveness of museums and places of worship.* Newcastle, UK: Cambridge Scholars Publishing.

—. 2009a. *American museums and the persuasive impulse: Architectural form and space as social influence.* Newcastle, UK: Cambridge Scholars Publishing.

—. 2009b. *Western European museums and visual persuasion: Art, edifice, and social influence.* Newcastle, UK: Cambridge Scholars Publishing.

—. 2011. *Compelling form: Architecture as visual persuasion.* Newcastle, UK: Cambridge Scholars Publishing.

Rosenfield, L. W. 1989. Central Park and the celebration of civic virtue. In *American rhetoric: Context and criticism,* ed. T. W. Benson, 221-266. Carbondale: Southern Illinois University Press.

Roth, L. M. 1993. *Understanding architecture: Its elements, history, and meaning.* New York: Harper Collins.

Runte, A. 2010. *National parks: The American experience,* 4th Ed. Lanham, MD: Taylor Trade Publishing.

Sacred Destinations. Home. http://www.sacred-destinations.com.

Salisbury Cathedral. Home. http://www.salisburycathedral.org.uk.

San Antonio River Walk. Home. http://www.thesanantionioriverwalk.com.

San Diego Zoo Safari Park. Home. http://www.sdzsafaripark.org.

San Francisco Recreation and Parks. Home. http://sfrecpark.org.

Scott, R. A. 2005. *The gothic enterprise; A guide to understanding the medieval cathedral.* Berkeley: University of California Press.

Senate Department for Urban Development and the Environment. Home. http://www.stadtenwicklung.berlin.de.

Sequoia National Park. Home. http://www.visitsequoia.com.

Smithsonian National Zoological Park. Home. http://nationalzoo.si.edu.

Southdale Center. Home. http://www.simon.com.

Steenburgen, C., and W. Reh. 2003. *Architecture and landcape: The design experiment of the great European gardens and landscapes,* Rev. ed. Basel: Birkhäuser Publishers.

Stiftung Preussische Schlösser und Gärten Berlin-Brandenburg. Home. http://www.spsg.de.

Stuart, R. 2010. *Gardens of the world: The great traditions.* London: Frances Lincoln Limited.

Strickland, C. 2001. *The annotated arch: A crash course in the history of architecture.* Kansas City, MO: Andrews McMeel Publishing.

Tange, A. K. 2004. Envisioning domesticity, locating identity: Constructing the Victorian middle class through images of home. In *Defining visual rhetorics,* ed. C. A. Hill and M. Helmers, 277-301. Mahwah, NJ: Lawrence Erlbaum.

Thacker, C. 1979. *The history of gardens.* Berkeley: University of California Press.

The National Mall. Home. http://www.nationalmall.org.

The Royal Parks. Home. http://www.royalparks.org.uk.

Tivoli. Home. http://www.tivoli.dk.

Trip Advisor. Home. http://www.tripadvisor.com.

Tung, A. M. 2003. *Preserving the world's great cities: The destruction and renewal of the historic metropolis.* New York: Three Rivers Press.

Universal Studios Orlando Resort. Home. http://www.universalorlando.com.

Urban Design: The Center for Design Excellence. Home. http://www.urbandesign.org.

Van Der Zanden, A. M., and S. N. Rodie. 2008. *Landscape design: Theory and application.* Clifton Park, NY: Thomson Delmar Learning.

Vandiver, F. E. 2002. *Civil War battlefields and landmarks,* Rev. Ed. Edison, NJ: Chartwell Books.

Vasaly, A. 1993. *Representations: Images of the world in Ciceronian oratory.* Berkeley: University of California Press.

Vitruvius, 1960. *The ten books on architecture.* Trans. M. H. Morgan. New York: Dover Publications.

Walt Disney World. Home. http://www.waltdisneyworld.com.

Wycherley, R. E. 1976. *How the Greeks built cities: The relationship of architecture and town planning to everyday life in ancient Greece.* New York: W. W. Norton.

York Minster. Home. http://www.yorkminster.org.

INDEX